THE AIRPORT BOOK

THE AIRPORT BOOK

From Landing Field to Modern Terminal

MARTIN GREIF

A Main Street Press Book
Published by Mayflower Books, Inc., U.S.A. New York

Library of Congress Catalog Card Number 79-2792
ISBN 8317-0150-1

Published by Mayflower Books, Inc., U.S.A.
575 Lexington Avenue, New York City 10022

Produced by The Main Street Press, Inc.
42 Main Street, Clinton, New Jersey 08809

Designed by Carl Berkowitz

Printed in the United States of America

Contents

"The City Airport," drawn for the United Aviation Corporation (United Airlines), 1928.

Preface

More often than not, the making of a book grows out of simple motives. I once wrote a book about architecture and design in the 1930s to counter the indiscriminate use of the term *Art Déco,* a term that didn't exist in its own day. The book grew out of a simple anger with the way many contemporary critics build upon the illogic of their own premises without ever taking the trouble to return to the historical source. No critic would dream of writing about, say, the 11th century without closely studying the documents of that period. But the recent past? That's another story altogether. We're still close enough to the '20s or '30s to feel superior to it. And too many of the period's survivors are still alive for us to be completely secure in our superiority. So, rather than ask them directly what their day was like, we dismiss them as old men, their memories wrapped in the cloak of senility. As to their written records, we ignore them as we ignore our own fathers. Unfortunately, we prefer our witnesses to history dead and, like every generation, we turn our backs on our fathers to make friends with our grandfathers.

As an avid reader of old magazines, I have learned to respect the past by attempting to understand its assessment of itself. (How many of my graduate school days at the Princeton library were ''wasted'' by poring over *New Yorker*s of the '20s and '30s rather than reading the florid (and horrid) 16th-century prose of John Lyly? And how many lunch hours at an early job at *The New York Times* were spent in the ''morgue'' reading the Sunday papers of fifty years ago? After reading a thousand old magazines and newspapers of an era of recent history, one begins to feel "comfortable" with the period and to comprehend our own romantic distortions of it.

The Airport Book is an attempt to reconstruct the past that has influenced our present. It has grown out of several motives, all of them simple. First, when a fascinating exhibition of "unbuilt architecture" was held in New York a few years ago, a story in *The New York Times* featured six or eight of the renderings of projects that for one reason or another had never been constructed. One of these was the plan for a rather grandiose airport terminal that had been designed in 1929. It was not only dismissed by the otherwise astute architectural critic of the *Times,* but was actually laughed at for looking more like a railroad terminal than an airport. "How silly!" was the judgment of the present. But it's all too easy to snigger at the past— especially if one doesn't understand it. And, in this case, at least, the *Times*'s critic didn't know that airports of the period *deliberately* attempted to look like railroad terminals in order to suggest to air-wary travelers the safety and comfort they associated with an older and accepted mode of transportation.

How I knew this bit of arcane information is the second strand that led to *The Airport Book.* At the time that the 1929 airport was ridiculed in the *Times,* I was researching a book on industrial architecture and came across photographs and renderings of some of the first airports built in America by The Austin Company of Cleveland, Ohio. The company's archives revealed that the first airports were designed consciously to resemble railroad terminals. Moreover, they were to serve as public parks as well. Some airports featured built-in stadiums for spectators; others had attached amusement parks and

swimming pools. Anything, in short, to attract a public that was simultaneously fascinated with "flying machines" and deathly afraid of ever "going up" in one. The railroad-station look was to suggest comfort and security. The public park idea was meant to bring out the crowds that would someday fly. And, in a day when aviation was hardly a profitable industry, amusement concessions from ferris wheels to swimming pools actually paid the rent.

So interesting were these early Austin airports that I tried—in vain, as I discovered— to find out more about them and other early airports from contemporary books. There are literally thousands of popular books in print on aviation, but almost every one of them concentrates on airplanes alone. One blockbuster of a book—the standard history of aviation, in fact—boasts an index of some 5,000 entries. There is not one listing for an airport!

Yet this is perfectly understandable. When I was a boy, a good number of Sundays in the 1940s were spent "watching the planes land." This was cheap family entertainment—all one needed was a car—and it was a way to keep three children occupied. So one Sunday it was Floyd Bennett Field; and another, La Guardia; and another, the biggest airport of them all—Idlewild. For some strange reason, we never watched the planes across the river in Newark. (Thirty-five years later this is still true of New Yorkers who would rather drive 30 miles due east than 10 miles into alien western territory—New Jersey.) As boys we went to see the planes, to watch them land and take off. Who cared about the dumb buildings? Perhaps as grown-up boys we buy nostalgic aviation books because all we really still care about are the planes. But what about those "dumb" buildings of our youths? They are, simply, no more. La Guardia, whose observation-deck telescopes swallowed dozens of my childhood nickles, was completely rebuilt twenty years ago; Idlewild was long ago subsumed by the first of the jet-age "airport cities," Kennedy International; and Floyd Bennett Field simply no longer exists. The third motive for *The Airport Book,* then, is nostalgia pure and simple. It attempts to explain why the past has been so quickly obliterated by the present.

Aviation has come so far in so short a time that we take for granted that airports have always been with us and that they have always been larger-than-life colossal structures, mazes of modern buildings filled with people so numbed by the familiarity of air travel that they no longer discern differences between one airport and another. *The Airport Book* takes us back to the meadow and prairie landing fields of 1911, when any flat field was an airport, and, in hundreds of provocative photographs covering a period of 70 years, suggests the development of an ever-changing form: the modern airport terminal.

Locating photographs of early airports has been anything but easy. We have always been far more interested in planes than in their hangars, and unphotogenic hangars were, unfortunately, the first "terminals." Even as commercial aviation developed in the '20s and '30s, photographers flocked to airports not to snap buildings or to immortalize other people gawking at the airplanes, but to photograph the planes themselves or the famous people who were arriving or departing in them. Most photographs of early airports, then, are really pictures of planes—with bits of buildings in the background. Still, with the help of a number of people and organizations—particularly regional historical societies—many previously unpublished treasures from the past have been unearthed. Although my sources are acknowledged separately at the end of the book, I am grateful for the assistance of several people whose dogged detective work went far beyond simple courtesy, personal or corporate: Rose Scotti of Trans World Airlines; M. J. Marinuk of Transport Canada; Samuel M. Jones of Doremus & Company; David Swindell of Scandinavian Airlines System; David A. Vine of the Aviation Department of Metropolitan Dade County, Florida; A. C. Maier-Neubert of the German Information Center; J. Daems of Sabena Belgian World Airlines; Nicholas Lorimer of the New Zealand Consulate General; Leo Pergament of the Board of Civil Aviation, Sweden; Eli Weisman of the Swedish Information Service; Marvin Epstein of The Austin Company; Allan S. Austin; and Mrs. Elmo Bruner. I am especially indebted to Jennifer Nadolski who coordinated the picture research by seeking out and contacting some 500 different sources. Finally, the citizens of Albuquerque, New Mexico, and Pueblo, Colorado, should be thanked for their foresight in having preserved their original airports as museums. May this spirit of recycling old buildings spread throughout the land.

Arriving at Atlanta International Airport.

Introduction

1. ATLANTA, 1928

A Sunday afternoon in Atlanta, Georgia: the year is 1928 and an American family has motored down to the Atlanta "air station," formerly a large open field on the old Candler estate. Although the man and his wife are still wedded to the terminology of the past, their eleven year old—proudly wearing his leather aviator's cap with goggles newly purchased from Sears, Roebuck—knows that the word "airport" has already begun to replace those pre-Lindbergh archaisms, "air stations," "airdrome," and "aerial garage." By the time the family arrives at the airport—a vast expanse of grass, punctuated by two small wooden hangars and an even smaller wooden shed for "air travelers"—a hundred automobiles or more have already parked in rows clear down to the edge of the landing field. More people will arrive as the day wears on. They will have come to watch, and to be thrilled by, landing and departing planes. Most will spend the day watching and waiting for the movement of an airplane, any airplane, and a hardy few will even venture into the air for a demonstration flight lasting ten minutes and providing a lifetime of stories to tell their grandchildren.

There are certain minimum basic requirements which all airports must have in this, the year after Lindbergh's flight from Roosevelt Field to Le Bourget, and Candler Field rates high on all of them. The landing field must be firm, approximately level, well drained, without obstructions or depressions which are hazardous in landing or taking off; or it must have at least two runways, 500 or more feet wide, crossing or converging at an angle of not less than 60 degrees to allow for take-offs

Candler Field (Atlanta Airport) in 1925: one hangar and 287 acres of grass.

in four different directions. If the sod is not sufficiently firm, the landing strips must be constructed of cinders, slag, or broken stone to prevent the aircraft from sinking in the mire in soggy weather.

Candler, one of the first in the country to boast two slag runways, is an ideal American flying field because it provides acre after acre of unobstructed open land. It is a favorite of experienced aviators who know firsthand that buildings, trees, towers, and any other obstructions on or adjacent to a landing field diminish the effective area of the field by seven times the height of the object. That is, if a flyer in making a landing must pass over and just clear a house 30 feet high, his plane will not touch the field until it is 210 feet from the house. Reversing the process, in order to clear the building on take-off, the plane (normally rising one foot in height for each seven feet it travels in a horizontal direction) would have to leave the field 210 feet or more from the building in order to clear it. But none of this presents any problem at Candler where the runways point in completely unobstructed directions and where the horizon is perfectly clear.

From the air, Candler is marked by a circle of whitewashed gravel well over 100 feet in diameter, with a band 4 feet wide around the circumference. And the name "Atlanta" is emblazoned in large white letters on the roof

Atlanta Airport in 1927: two hangars and two 1500-foot runways.

of one of the hangars, the letters readable at the height of 2,000 feet. For daytime visibility the runways are marked along the borders with 4-foot white circles constructed of whitewashed gravel or crushed rock and spaced about 25 feet apart. Its white markers glistening in the afternoon sun, Candler Field is, all in all, the very model of a 1928 American airport and a far cry from the golf courses and baseball parks that still pass for airports in most of the country. The buildings are lamentably few and small and rather rickety. But who has come to gawk at buildings? The plane's the thing!

The three o'clock plane from Macon—a Ford Tri-motor—has just touched down with a roar, its three propellers raising a cloud of dust and cinders. Men clutch their hats and women their short skirts, but all are far too excited by the miraculous landing of this heavier-than-air marvel, the ultimate wonder of an age of wonders, to be concerned about the discomfort of the momentary dust storm. A man in white coveralls places the wheel chocks in position and the whirring airscrews finally come to a stop. Six passengers are discharged—two waving to the crowd and at least one looking somewhat pale—and then mail and packages follow from the hold in the fuselage. After a time, when the mail bags and express parcels are placed on a waiting truck, the plane is taxied to a hangar, the

Atlanta Municipal Airport, c. 1931: the airport as railroad terminal.

engine is shut off, and the pilot, removing his goggles and unhooking his parachute, climbs down from his ship. After the plane has been moved into the hangar, it is carefully inspected by mechanics, repaired if necessary, refueled, and made ready for the next trip. Another plane, reversing the process, takes on passengers, mail, and express matter, receives a "go-ahead" in semaphore from the flagman, taxies to a favorable position on the field, and takes off into the direction of the wind. The crowd of spectators cheers.

The weather observer, a busy and important adjunct to the airport, takes and records the readings of the thermometers, barometer, wind direction and velocity, clouds and visibility. He sends up a minature hydrogen balloon, and by means of a stopwatch and a theodolite takes observations on the location of the balloon at one-minute intervals. This enables him to determine the velocity of the wind at various elevations above the earth's surface. All weather reports and observations made at the airport, and those received by radio from other weather stations, are posted on a large bulletin board in the aviators' room. Meanwhile, the airport's post office, where men sort the mail that has just arrived and process the bags to be shipped out on the next flight, is as busy and as completely equipped as the office in a fair-sized city. It is the success of the Air Mail Service, of course,

Atlanta Municipal Airport, c. 1939.

that has made commercial passenger flight possible in America.

As evening approaches, spectators dine from picnic baskets on the grass or from the running boards of their Hupmobiles or Packards, knowing that the tiny airport restaurant cannot possibly feed the multitudes that have come to watch the planes at night. For at night the airport, with its many sharp lights, is like a startling modern stage setting. Each light has its own meaning and important use. There are the white boundary lights marking the limits of the field, green lights marking the runways, red warning lights on obstructions such as tops of towers, telegraph poles, or buildings. The rotating beacon,

operated from sunset to sunrise, points its finger of light into the sky as a guide to the pilot. The floodlights give an even distribution of light over the field, enabling the pilot to select his landing place, and the illuminated wind-direction indicator gives him the best direction for landing. The apparent ease with which the pilot makes a night landing is remarkable. All the airport lights are turned on shortly before the plane is expected. The drone of the motor is heard in the distance, and soon, out of the darkness, the green and red lights—marking the right and left wing tips—and the white tail lights, become visible. These three lights approach the field, pass over the wind-direction cone, and move to a

Atlanta Municipal Airport in 1948: 1230 acres and a postwar terminal.

position pointing into the wind. A small pencil of light shoots downward from the plane to the field. Out of the darkness and into the illuminated zone of the floodlights, comes the plane. In a swirl of wind and dust, it swoops down to the field and the "hop" is ended.

2. LONDON, 1928

After eight years of experience in transport aviation, the airport for London at Croydon is one of the best-equipped and operated air terminals in the world. The new Croydon, which was formally dedicated in May, 1928, by Lady Maude Hoare, is a vast improvement over the old airport that had been used regularly by all transport planes operating between England and the Continent since the Great War.

This airport is located about 12 miles from the heart of London, its supporting metropolis. The Air Ministry, Britain's controlling air body, is responsible for the improvements that have been effected. The old field, although successfully used since 1920, was considered too small for the extensive operations that were taking place daily, and because of this lack of area, considerable difficulty was experienced in the control of aircraft landing and taking off. Still, the old Croydon was an improvement over the field at Hounslow Heath where air service between London and Paris had been inaugurated on

Atlanta Municipal Airport, c. 1962: 3900 acres and skyrocketing traffic.

August 25, 1919, by Aircraft Transport & Travel Limited. That first flight had carried a single passenger.

In line with Croydon's improvement program, the old airport buildings were either torn down or moved in order that the additional property to be utilized could be made a part of the old field. The new Croydon boasts an effective operating area of slightly over 4,000 feet in all directions from a field that is nearly an exact square. The landing area is tile drained and is entirely of a deep-rooted turf that stands up excellently, even during the protracted wet spells that prevail during certain periods of the year. Leveling and rolling machinery is a part of the airport equipment

and is used to keep the field smooth and in condition.

According to authorities there is no necessity for hard-surfaced runways and none are contemplated. Everyone knows that pilots prefer firm turf and that talk of paved airstrips is just that—talk. Officials in charge of the control of operations are of the opinion that the regulation of traffic is much easier from an all-way field than from an airport having a definite runway system. Since the modern aircraft of 1928 are almost as sensitive to cross winds as were their primitive ancestors of only a few years ago, Croydon prefers a plan whereby a large pad in the middle of the grass landing field allows the planes

Atlanta's Central Passenger Terminal Complex: world's largest airport.

to head in any direction for take-off or landing. A large concrete apron, however, has been provided for aircraft and cargo. After warming the engines at a distance so as not to annoy the sensibilities of air travelers, the plane about to take on passengers is towed to the concrete loading area in front of the administration building.

The main buildings at Croydon consist of an administration building, four large hangars, repair shops, and a hotel. Unlike the sorry wooden structures in America, these are solid in appearance and give a feeling of permanence. They seem to say in masonry and steel that the infancy of aviation is over and that the airplane is here to stay. The administration building is a long, low structure, and except for the control tower does not exceed two stories in height. This building is as complete in detail as is the modern railway station. Every convenience is included for the comfort of the air traveler. The large waiting room provides comfortable seats for those awaiting departure. A bulletin board shows the schedule of departures and arrivals of all airplanes engaged in regular operations over scheduled routes, and a large weather map shows wind directions and heights of clouds. Ticket offices are conveniently placed as are telegraph and telephone facilities and also a branch post office and an express office. Customs and immigration officials occupy space in this building, and their examinations are carried out promptly with little confusion. The office rooms of the various operating transport companies are conveniently located; airline attachés are on hand to answer inquiries and render such services as the air traveler may require.

The control tower rises over the center of the building and is two stories higher. From this tower is carried out the system of control of airplanes in the air. It is as modern as 1928. Reports are received and transmitted, and regular meteorological information is broadcast to airplanes while in flight. Two-way communication is carried on at regular intervals, and, by radio triangulation during fog, definite information is at all times available as to the actual position of aircraft en route.

The hangars, each 330 feet by 150 feet, are of concrete construction with supporting trusses and girders of steel. Adjoining them are workshops and storerooms from which may be obtained all types of spare parts and maintenance equipment. Each hangar is equipped with an overhead crane of 4,000-pound capacity which greatly expedites a major overhaul of engine or airplane. The facilities that are provided allow several separate repair jobs to go forward at the same time.

The airport hotel is located just north of the administration building and, though not large in size, is a very popular and useful adjunct. It contains a restaurant and a reading and lounge room, all of which are extensively used by patrons of the airport. Rooms are available for those wishing to stay at the airport overnight in order that an early start may be obtained in the morning. An attractive and most popular feature of the hotel in summer is a wide terrace between it and the airplane-loading area. This terrace is provided with

tables and colored umbrellas, and refreshments and full meals are served out-doors in full view of the aircraft. The hotel is quite a gathering place for groups and individuals engaged in the aviation industry or who are interested in various phases of aeronautics. In fact, the hotel has proved so popular that enlargement to double the present size is planned. Croydon, however, cannot hope to compete with Tempelhof's facilities for spectators, where thousands of Berliners can dine in comfort while watching the activities on the landing field, but it does offer first-class service for its passengers and their guests.

The lighting equipment that has been installed at Croydon is rather elaborate and is quite a departure from the methods used in the United States. Landing lights are sunk in the field to denote the landing direction. These lights show the direction of the prevailing wind and can be automatically changed by remote control from the tower. A red neon beacon is used to penetrate the fog that rolls in on occasion. A mobile floodlight unit has been installed on a specially designed motor truck and is used to floodlight that part of the airport on which a night landing is to be made. Fixed red lights are mounted on all obstructions, and the outline of the airport is indicated by flashing red lights mounted on 4-foot standards.

The "despatch office" or passenger terminal is of special interest. Here we see people who have just arrived; only a few hours ago they were in the capital of another country. Contrary to what one might think, they do not wear fur coats, since air travel is not at all the frigid mode of transportation that it once was; nor do they appear to have come through a grueling experience. There in the handcart is their heavy luggage; regular government customs officers are superintending the examination; immigration officials are examining the passports; and in less than ten minutes the passengers roll away to their hotels in special motor buses belonging to Imperial Airways.

From the despatch office we also see passengers about to leave for Berlin, Cologne, Brussels, or Paris. About ten minutes before departure, passengers at the Imperial Airways office in the administration building are given a little pamphlet which they are requested to read. It contains a few notes with the following helpful suggestions:

Special clothing is not necessary for air travel. Clothing suitable for a motor car journey is adequate. Maps of routes can be obtained free at the aerodrome before departure. Do not be concerned if the machine on starting taxies slowly towards a corner of the aerodrome. An aeroplane always starts and lands head against the wind. After a small run the machine almost imperceptibly rises from the ground. We recommend passengers to place cotton-wool in their ears to deafen the noise caused by the engines. Slight deafness is sometimes caused by atmospheric pressure, and immediate relief can be obtained by either just blowing your nose, with the nostrils pinched together, or, when landing, by going through the action of swallowing. In order to turn, an aeroplane banks— one side is raised above the horizontal and the other side lowered. This is a perfectly safe movement.

"Air pockets" do not exist, and when "bumps" occur they are caused by upward and downward currents of air, which have a similar effect on aeroplanes as waves do on ships.

Dizziness, as experienced by some people when looking down from a high building, is unknown in aeroplanes, as there is no connection with the earth.

Air sickness affects fewer passengers than sea sickness; passengers say that the finest cure for sea sickness is fresh air.

The windows of the cabin can be opened or shut as desired. Every aeroplane is fitted with an emergency exit in the roof of the cabin. It is clearly marked as such and will open when pulling the ring attached to it.

In case of sickness receptacles are provided and kept in the left back corner of the cabin. Do not throw these receptacles out of the machine.

Passengers need have no cause for alarm when hearing the engines slowing down; this is only an indication that the pilot is preparing to land, and he wishes to reduce speed, or that he desires to fly at a lower altitude which may, in his opinion, be advisable owing to calmer weather or better visibility, etc.

All Imperial machines flying on Continental scheduled services have lavatory accommodations at the rear of the cabin, and passengers can freely move about the cabin without affecting the balance of the aeroplane.

Drinking water and glasses are carried on all Imperial machines.

It is prohibited by Government Regulations to smoke or light matches in the aeroplane.

Nothing whatsoever should be thrown out of the windows of the aeroplane.

In the case of necessity, passengers can communicate with the pilot through the aperture in front of the cabin.

Your pilot is in constant touch with his Terminal aerodrome by means of wireless telephony. He receives reports regarding the weather conditions at frequent intervals, and can ask for any information he needs at any time.

Reassured, the passengers await their "machines." Now the station master calls out the destination of the next airplane to depart. The flight tickets are examined, the baggage weighed; then off to the airplane into whose fuselage an uncanny pile of freight and trunks vanish; the engines are set going and quickly tested once more, and then the blocks in front of the wheels are taken away. There is a shout, "Blocks off!" The machine taxies to the starting position and takes off at an "All clear" signal from the air-control officer, eventually to land at Le Bourget in a little less than two and a half hours.

3. LONDON AND ATLANTA, 1979

Croydon Airport is no more. As one writer put it in 1968, "it is a sign of the times that Croydon now lies as a wasting green expanse just outside the town that it helped prosper and has been shouldered aside by the ever-growing London airports at Heathrow and Gatwick which are large, costly, and slick to serve the traffic that now runs into thousands instead of dozens every weekday." But that was 1968. As it enters the 1980s, Heathrow alone accommodates some 30 million passengers—or an average of 86,000 passengers a day, visiting relatives and friends not included.

As if anyone needed to tell us, we are living in the jet age. Almost everyone flies today. And why not? With long-distance train travel a luxury for those who have the time, and with ocean liners as extinct as the dinosaur, what choice does the traveler have? During the first decade of the jet age, airport planners used to worry most about overcrowded skies and overtaxed runways. Jumbo jets, carrying twice as many passengers as previous planes,

solved that problem, but created a new one: dealing with the tens of thousands of people who surge through a terminal whenever several of the big planes are landing or taking off at about the same time. In a superb article in *The Wall Street Journal,* the writer Jane Kronholz paints a grim picture of the current "jumbo jumble" at Heathrow, but the scene might just as well be New York's Kennedy International Airport, or the terminals in Los Angeles, Chicago, Hong Kong, Sydney, Nairobi, or elsewhere as our aging "airport cities" of the '60s reach their saturation points:

When the jumbos arrive in force at Heathrow, or depart from it, lines lengthen at check-in counters, control points, and baggage-claim areas, while waiting rooms and coffee shops fill with travelers and their friends and relatives. "Some days there are so many bodies lying about waiting for planes that you can't get to the lunch buffet," says one airline worker. "Then the children get hungry and start to cry, the mothers get upset, the fathers get angry, and you have a bloody mess."

Other factors don't help. The baggage conveyors and the computers that control certain equipment sometimes don't work. The moving sidewalks sometimes don't move. Only a few airlines have baggage X-rays, so security checks are done the hard way, by hand.

Arriving passengers need at least 40 minutes after disembarking to clear government controls and claim their baggage, although waits of two hours aren't uncommon....

At times last winter, the congestion grew so bad that airlines couldn't unload their arriving passengers. [Some had to wait two hours to get off their flights.] Airlines using Heathrow routinely tell departing passengers to check in two hours before flight time, but on one occasion airport officials banned furious travelers from entering the terminals until 45 minutes before their flight time to prevent anticipated congestion. But is it fair to blame the airport for failing to keep up with the "future shock" developments of aeronautics? Architectural critic Wolf Von Eckardt predicted the dilemma of the jet-age airport fifteen years ago: "Even if we suddenly . . . started to build properly located and designed airports, it would take five years at the very least before the first plane could land in them. By that time, the experts say, present airline passenger traffic—which already carries more people than our buses and trains combined—will have doubled. In another five years it will have doubled again." Given that rate of growth, how could any airport—new or old—be anything but overcrowded?

The problem at Heathrow is that, when it was converted from military use after World War II, it was added to and added to again and again in an attempt to keep up with changing aircraft technology. Now, of course, it resembles a very cleverly arranged house of cards. Designed in 1946 as a unit of terminals placed within a star formed by the runways, the airport is an unwilling captive of a long-outdated plan. And there is no room for further expansion. Although access to a new terminal building may be gained by tunneling passengers under an active runway, even this ingenious solution will gain Heathrow only a temporary breather. The growth of air travel in the 1980s makes certain that this new terminal will be outgrown as soon as it is built. Clearly, London will need a third international airport long before the 21st century.

London needs a new airport, but Atlanta has one. Candler Field has grown through the years into the William B. Hartsfield Atlanta International Airport—the second busiest air terminal in the world, second only to Chicago's O'Hare. Of the more than 30 million passengers who enplaned or deplaned at Atlanta in 1977, 72 percent were transfer passengers, making Atlanta the largest transfer hub in the world. But with such spectacular growth has come the usual problem of the '70s: terminals bursting at the seams. To accommodate passengers of the '80s, Atlanta is building an entirely new terminal, which, when it opens in late 1980, will be the world's largest and most modern. The new buildings of the Central Passenger Terminal Complex will occupy an area of 378.5 acres, an area 31 percent greater than that which the entire Candler Field—runways and all—occupied in 1928. The $327 million terminal will be capable initially of handling 104 wide-bodied airplanes, an increase of 32 over the present terminal's capacity for all aircraft. There is room for an additional 26-gate concourse to be constructed when needed.

The enormous complex consists of two main terminal buildings, four concourses (to accommodate the high percentage of Atlanta's transfer passengers), and a "people mover mall"—an underground transit system connecting the terminals to the concourses. Considering the Brobdingnagian size of the terminal complex (2.2 million square feet of usable space or the equivalent of seven 24-story block-square office buildings—an area more than 11 times that of a football field), an incredible system of moving sidewalks and a Westinghouse Automated Guideway Transit System (AGTS) has been devised to make excessive walking—the modern travelers' bane—an all but unknown complaint. The AGTS consists of 17 vehicles —each carrying 80 passengers—that transport passengers around a two-mile reverse turn-back loop connecting the terminal building with each of the four concourses. Even Jacques Tati, who in his film *Playtime* satirized jet-age terminals as boring at best and sterile at worst, would find the concept fascinating.

Although they realize that the Central Passenger Terminal Complex will ease airport congestion for some time to come, the planners of Hartsfield-Atlanta are not at all complacent. With the number of passengers and air traffic steadily increasing, completion of the complex will not end future airport development. Plans are presently underway to construct an additional concourse, extend the Automated Guideway Transit System to serve the concourse, add and extend runways, develop a new mid-field support area, including air cargo, catering, and postal facilities.

No airport ever built has been considered "finished" or "complete," Atlanta and Heathrow included. Few travelers, in fact, have ever passed through an air terminal that was free of the sound of laborers' jackhammers. The airport is an ever-changing form, defying permanence. No airport ever built, in fact, has ever been completely up-to-date and all may be said to remain in a continuous state of redevelopment from the day that they open. That this has been true since the dawn of commercial aviation is the primary subject of the pages that follow.

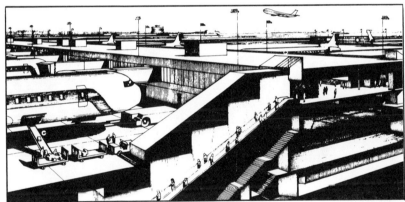

Atlanta's new Central Passenger Terminal Complex.

In 1919, after a German baron's estate in Louisville, Kentucky, was confiscated under the Alien Property Act, A. H. Bowman leased 50 acres for an airfield. This cornfield evolved into Bowman Field, one of America's earliest airports.

1
Touching Down: Meadows, Fairgrounds, Country Clubs, and Cemeteries

Before there were airports there were landing fields. And before there were landing fields there were simply open stretches of land—anywhere that the early spider-like flying machines could alight: farmers' fields, pastures, the lawns of resort hotels and country clubs, or even the grassy expanse of the local golf course.

At the end of World War I—fifteen years after the Wright Brothers' flight at Kitty Hawk—the United States Army Air Service listed 980 official landing fields in America. A study of this list discloses some astonishing facts. One of these is that there were then only thirteen municipal flying fields in the entire country. Another is that the early aviator was likely to be considered an intruder, even if a welcome one, at almost any field on which he might alight in America.

There were forty-four government-owned landing places in the United States, including those for "water machines," but in all other fields listed, aside from the baker's dozen of municipal fields, the "flying man" of 1918 could not be certain that the folks below would be ready for him if he decided to—or, indeed, *had* to—alight on their property.

On twenty-eight of the Army's list of landing fields the pilot would very likely have broken up a golf game, to say the least, for twenty-eight golf and country clubs had given the government permission to list their grounds and courses as official landing places. One contemporary critic was quick to point out the insanity of this practice: "To the layman who has never flown, a golf course seems an ideal landing place. There is usually plenty of space, with lots of grassy spots and smooth ground. The layman, indeed, might be justified in saying: 'What's all this bother about landing fields? Every town in America has got a golf course. Why not make the course in every town the official landing place there and mark it out in white so the flyers'll see it? That way you'll soon have a string of landing places running in every direction from every city and town in the United States. I know my club would vote a welcome to flyers, and we'd be glad to entertain 'em in our clubhouse.' The truth about golf courses as landing places, however, is that they are about as safe as Pikes Peak. From even a small height the flyer cannot see the grass-covered ridges and bunkers and barricades that are the pride of every good course. Below him the earth stretches out treacherously green and smooth. But death lurks on the links for a flyer. The chances are that, the very moment his wheels touch earth, he will find himself racing, in automobile fashion, straight up against a grass-covered wall of earth that will dash him to injury. More than this, there are few long straightways on any golf course for either landing or starting. If there is a deep-set brook or ravine in the neighborhood of a town, the links are built up around it, so that the players must cross it three or four times—the more times the better. The hazards of a course means only a challenge and tight, hard playing to the man with a golf stick, but to the man in an aeroplane they mean the hazard of disaster."

Of the remaining fields on the Army list of 1918, thirty-eight were race tracks. Of these, nine were half-mile tracks with room enough for a flyer to alight, but not room enough to take off again, unless a high wind and perfect conditions happened to be the pilot's good fortune. In addition to race-track landing fields, sixteen county fairgrounds were on the list, but not one of them was marked as "good" or "safe." The aviator using the list, in fact, would have been advised to use these fairgrounds as a landing place only in the case of an "emergency."

Two "baseball grounds" were on the list. One of them, described as an ideal flying field "on days when there is no game," was a third of a mile square. The other, 800 feet long and 100 feet wide, was far too small—even in 1918—for either a landing or a take-off unless the wind were coming from exactly the right direction, but this limitation didn't prevent its inclusion as an official airfield. In addition to the two ball parks, several polo fields were listed, one of them being New York's famous Polo Grounds, far better known as a baseball stadium than for its original purpose, but still surrounded in 1918 by open countryside. Curiously, the Army list makes no mention of a three-story obstruction at this "emergency" landing station: the Ninth Avenue Elevated Railway located directly behind the playing field.

Among its more unusual recommendations, the official government list of "aerial garages" mentions two Nevada towns that made use of nearby lake beds, gone dry, and one of these strange landing fields was even marked on the government records as "good." (One can only surmise what a poor landing field must have been like.) In addition, there were listed two county poor farms in Illinois, one old soldiers' home in the same state, an insane asylum outside Detroit, and even a cemetery in the state of Michigan. (One imagines that the cemetery must have been a memorial park—a burial ground without tombstones—but the Army list is strangely silent on this point.) A contemporary joke, however, is more humorously explicit. Early pilots, apparently, had a favorite definition of a landing field.

According to them, it was "a small and uneven open space surrounded on three sides by telephone and telegraph lines and blocked on the fourth by a graveyard." If a pilot, crazy enough to fly in the first place, flew too low from one direction, he'd hit the wires. And if he crashed on the fourth side, he'd be right where he belonged—in the graveyard.

Race tracks, polo fields, golf courses, open fields. These were the first "air stations," both in America and in Europe (Berlin's famed Tempelhof was originally a military parade ground, as was Le Bourget in Paris, and air meets were frequently held at race courses in England and in Ireland). But if this was the reality of aviation in its fledgling years, the dreamers were already envisioning the *planned* landing field of the future—open spaces carefully sited and incorporating standards rigidly set by national aviation agencies and administered by municipal government. "A dozen years from now," one flying enthusiast wrote in 1919, "when excellent and fully equipped flying fields will be found all over the world, and when air traffic will have shaped its course along the route laid out by enterprising cities which were leaders in the establishment of municipal landing fields, then any mention of 'Si Jones's Field,' or 'a cotton patch two miles east of town,' or 'Swenson's Farm,' will be an interesting relic of aviation's history."

What goes up. . .

A Curtiss biplane rising from an unidentified American field, c. 1911.

. . . *must come down.*

The wreck of the first airplane flown in Hawaii, 1912. The pilot had ascended 40 feet.

Many early airplanes, built in home workshops, were wheeled directly from the barn to the pasture for test runs. Whether the c. 1906 craft above ever flew is not known. *Right:* The Curtiss-Wright plane on an open field in Tucson, Arizona, in 1912 suggests the excitement and novelty of early aviation. That any of these spectators were even dimly aware of the possibilities of heavier-than-air powered flight as more than merely a dangerous sport is doubtful.

Preparing to take off from a field in Tucson, Arizona, pioneer aviator Charles K. Hamilton's biplane suggests a passage in S. P. Cockerell's "Aerodrome Reflections" (1912): "The invention of the aeroplane will stand out in the history of the 20th century as conspicuously as the invention of the locomotive did in the history of the 19th. The unwieldy, medieval-looking machines in use today, crudely simple, like Nature's own early attempts at winged life, will arouse the same sense of pity and admiration that we experience on comparing 'Puffing Billy' with the modern railway engine."

Opposite: The first military flying fields were used for balloons, important instruments of defense during World War I employed both for reconnaissance flights and for anti-aircraft "barrages." With steel wires trailing earthward like flexible teeth in an enormous comb, an obstructing balloon could force an attacking airplane to rise above it—to a height from which no bomb could then be accurately aimed—or dive below it—and risk point-blank anti-aircraft fire. Recorded here are cadets in training at Camp Wheeler, Macon, Georgia, and soldiers making miniature balloons at the U.S. Balloon School of the Signal Corps, Fort Sill, Oklahoma.

Before World War I, Glenn Curtiss wrote that "marine flying will be developed quicker than land—because there are no landing fields needed. Terminal facilities are already provided—the surface of the water itself." *Upper right:* Richard C. Saufley at the controls of a Curtiss AH pusher hydroaeroplane at the Naval Air Station, Pensacola, Florida, 1914. *Above:* An unidentified pilot demonstrates that shallow water presents no obstacle to floatplanes.

In one of the last letters that Wilbur Wright was to pen before his death in 1912, he wrote that "the real problem now confronting us is to find out whether we too, like the birds—once we are in the air—can stay in it indefinitely. The bird can do it. Why can't men?" Less than four years later, on June 9, 1916, Richard C. Saufley (p. 33), at the controls of a Curtiss AH-9 hydroaeroplane, crashed to his death off Pensacola, Florida, after an endurance flight lasting eight hours and 51 minutes. Surely, man was closer to his goal of imitating the "indefinite" flight of birds, but, just as surely, places for safe landing would always be necessary if paying passengers were to be coaxed into the air. Within the next decade, cities and

towns, no matter how densely populated or remotely located, would provide similar landing facilities for pioneering aviators. If an area boasted an open body of water or a well-drained stretch of level, grassy land, it could be employed as an "air-sea base" or as an "aerial garage." *Top:* Pilots Roy Davis and Russ Merrill arriving at remote Yakutat, Alaska, 1925. *Above:* Valdez, Alaska, which became an important military base during World War II, provided an open flying field in the 1920s. *Opposite page:* Three views of the grassy landing field at Bismarck, North Dakota, 1927-28. The plane at the bottom is a 12-passenger Ford Tri-motor.

Top: A Ford Tri-motor at the Lexington (Kentucky) Airport, which in the late '20s was still the field of an old farm.

Above: Sporting togs for the aviator of 1924. If the pilot was forced to put down on the grounds of a country club, he was at least suitably dressed for the links.

This page: Biplanes putting down on open fields without runways in the mid-'20s. Forced landings were not rare in the early days of flying, and to overcome the lack of designated landing fields, it was imperative that landing speeds be slow, requiring little space in such emergencies.

Well after paved runways were developed, pilots still preferred turf. Grass offered resiliency on landing, provided a grip for the tail skid, thereby acting as a break, and, since there were no definite lanes to follow, allowed take-offs and landings in any desired direction. *Below:* A Ford Tri-motor at the Mt. Plymouth (Florida) Hotel and Golf Course, c. 1929.

Opposite: Even as these photographs were taken, primitive landing fields were on the verge of development. Planned landing sites were soon to replace the open field. *Left:* The Governor of Kentucky, Flem Sampson, about to take off from the old Frankfort field while the municipal airport is under construction, 1928. *Right:* The Governor of Iowa, John Hammill, at an air show in Centerville, 1929.

Delivering the mail, Honolulu, Hawaii, 1926.

2
The Dawn of Commercial Aviation: The First Landing Fields

In 1920 William G. Shepherd, an American journalist with a particular interest in aviation, wrote an eloquent plea to an indifferent public arguing for the development of "wide, safe landing fields for the flyers of the future." Since this writer's name seems never to have been preserved in any history of aviation, it seems proper to quote in full one of his more elaborate similes. Neither before nor since, one imagines, has the airport been likened to a bird house:

"An airplane can do almost everything that a bird can do, except build its own nest. There are birds that, in addition to building their nests, trample down the grass and weeds around their homes to give themselves a stamping ground. The airplane that tries to trample down trees and saplings that surround its nesting place hurts itself grievously. 'Bird houses' for airplanes, and stamping grounds on which they may either alight or make their long swift runs that carry them into the air, are as necessary for airplanes as nests are for birds. There is a great society of bird lovers, made up of householders, who devise bird houses which are intended to attract birds. The Audubon Society knows every domestic whim or every desirable American bird, and no farm home is complete without its neat little home for birds. What we need today is an Audubon Society of American cities and towns for the cultivation of the welfare of our linen-winged, aluminum-lunged, unfeathered friends. Whether we have bird houses scattered over the country or not, real birds will still survive, though we may not be able to coax them to our particular neighborhood. But the motor-driven, linen-winged birds cannot be born in great numbers and cannot carry out the promises of their great future unless bird houses dot our land and stamping grounds spread over the country at no very great distances apart.''

At the same time that Shepherd was likening airfields to bird houses in his attempt to convince Americans of the need for safe landing facilities in their towns and cities, Holt Thomas, the most imposing figure in British aviation and the president of the Aircraft Manufacturing Co., Ltd., the firm which built the famous De Haviland planes of World War I, had a vision of his own: ''The commercial machine,'' he wrote, ''must always be within touch not necessarily of an aerodrome but of an alighting ground. My idea is that there should be landing grounds every ten miles throughout the world, with wireless or telephone means of communication with depots, so that if your plane came down through engine failure, all that the pilot would have to do would be to telephone the nearest depot, 'I am down with engine failure on Ground 8,' and within a very short period a fresh machine and a fresh pilot would be speeding to his assistance.''

What was spurring the demand for planned landing fields, or air stations as they were sometimes called, was the almost worldwide acceptance of air mail, inaugurated in the United States with the New York, Philadelphia, and Washington mail flight of May 15, 1918, and then instituted in most European cities from Berlin to Munich, from Vienna to Budapest, from Rome to Brindisi, from Madrid to Barcelona, from London to Paris, from Paris to Lyons, to Marseilles, to Nice, to Corsica. ''Very few persons realize what an undertaking that is,'' wrote Otto Praeger, the American postmaster in charge

of the Aerial Mail System in 1919. ''Never has a trip by air been undertaken whereby a ship leaves for an 800-mile voyage, one each way, a day, flying over mountains with very few landing places—an undertaking which six months ago would have been regarded absolutely impossible.'' Postmaster Praeger was referring to the New York to Chicago leg of the transcontinental air-mail line. Trial flights had shown him that it was possible to make the distance in nine hours, beating the fastest train by twelve. Five landing fields and emergency stops had been established at Lehighton, Bellefonte, and Clarion, Pennsylvania, and at Cleveland and Bryan, Ohio, making the journey a series of 150-mile hops. At each of these fields was a hangar, an extra airplane, an extra aviator, and supplies and mechanics, while at the Chicago end of the flight was a $15,000 hangar donated by the businessmen of that city. The role of local businessmen in the establishment of airfields was realized as crucial, for if air-mail service proved successful, and if passenger service, as predicted, were soon to follow, then business in general stood most to gain if commercial aviation could be made profitable. Farsighted critics, therefore, began to appeal to businessmen and to civic leaders to provide sites for municipal air stations in order to prevent any fledgling airline companies from developing transportation monopolies as the railroads had done in the 19th century.

By 1923 or '24, the ideal air-terminal site was to allow provision for both land and water types of aircraft. For land types a square plot of 2,000 by 2,000 feet was considered satisfactory. For seaplane bases only a small plot was necessary, about 500 feet of waterfront, by 500 feet wide, adjacent to a clear water surface of about 3,000 by 4,000 feet, or connected with it by a channel about 250 to 600 feet wide. Seaplane bases did not require that this stretch of water be particularly deep—only 4 feet was considered sufficient to provide draft for the seaplane or flying boat of the mid-'20s.

The ideal landing field of the 1920s was perhaps best described in 1923 by Archibald Black, an aeronautical engineer:

In general, a square plot is the most suitable for the terminal. Runways should be arranged so that airplanes can land on or take off from them directly into the wind the greatest possible part of the time. For ordinary airplanes and for sea-level altitudes, they should be about 2,500 to 3,000 feet long. Unless the soil drains particularly well, some attention should be given to artificial drainage, particularly around the runways. It is advisable to surface the most-used portions of the runways with gravel, cinders, or other available material unless the soil drains very well. The ends should be kept clear of obstructions. All ditches should be filled up to the level of the field. the hangars, gasoline house, and all other buildings should be well spaced to reduce the fire hazard, and some suitable fire-extinguishing apparatus should be provided for. The immediate requirements will usually be very modest. The important point is to obtain the site and prepare plans for its eventual development along comprehensive lines. In many cases, one hangar, some means of storing gasoline and oil, a wind indicator, telephone connection, and a location marker will be all that are necessary in the way of equipment.

The early flying field, then, was still a good-sized meadow, rough and dusty with a poor grade of grass, if any. There might have been a row of high-gabled frame buildings along one side. There usually was some sort of primitive wind-direction indicator, but few surfaced runways, no lighting, no traffic control to worry about, and no weather bulletins. Just a field. That was all that was needed. It suited the age of aviator goggles and riding jodhpurs. But of these simple beginnings, the idea of the modern airport was born.

Different possible arrangements of air terminals, 1923.

Opposite, top: Photographed in 1912 from a B-2 Wright biplane, the airfield in Cicero, Illinois, was operated by the Aero Club of Illinois and was considered the largest and most complete field in the United States. Part of the 1912 International Air Meet was held here. A row of hangars appears along the edge of the field, and at the end of the hangars are the administration buildings. In the foreground are machine shops. *Opposite, bottom:* Typical of military installations during World War I, the airfield at North Island, San Diego, California, was furnished with wooden hangars and headquarters. Even if more permanent structures had been wanted, a worldwide steel shortage would have made such construction impossible.

Above: The first hangars in Elko, Nevada, were erected to accommodate air-mail service in 1920. The structure on the left seems to have been built of barn siding; the hangar on the right is a canvas tent.

The seaplane tent hangars (*top*) that
inaugurated the Naval Air Station at
Pensacola, Florida, in 1914 were replaced the
following year by masonry structures, several
of which are still in use some years later. In
the 1918 photograph (*above*), note the
Curtiss H-12L flying boats with roundels on
the wings.

The Curtiss H-16 flying boats,
introduced by the U.S. Navy in 1917 and sold
in knockdown condition to Britain, where
they were known as "Large Americas,"
weighed almost 11,000 pounds and carried a
crew of four, six Lewis machine guns, and
four 230-pound bombs. Still, a Navy crew
could haul it manually from the water to its
hangar.

Opposite: Lambert Field in St. Louis, Missouri, grew into one of America's busiest airports. In 1921, its single improvement was an all-purpose wooden hangar. *Top:* The typical hangar of the early 1920s was garage, repair shop, assembly plant, and fueling station rolled into one. *Above:* A 60X Moth at the Calgary (Alberta) Aero Club in 1928 partially obscures its hangar, built in part from the packing cases in which such aircraft were shipped from England.

ROUTES

84,771 MILES DAILY
ES OF AIRWAYS

If war sped the development of aviation technology, then the needs of business in peacetime led to the first demands made for improved landing facilities. The universal success of air-mail service, after slow starts in Europe and in the Americas, resulted in the necessity of safe landing "ports" for mail planes in even the most remote places. Against the backdrop of a 1927 map of U.S. Air-Mail routes is seen (*far left, top*) a De Haviland DH-4 mail plane in Alaska, (*far left, bottom*) mail being delivered to a dog team on Alaska's Kuskokwim River, and (*left*) mail planes at Reno, Nevada, in 1920. The Alaskan pilot in both 1925 photos is Carl Ben Eilson. Until the development of "super" passenger planes in the late 1930s, snow-covered fields presented no problem for landings so long as the plane was on skis.

The earliest structures on early flying fields were undoubtedly buildings that were acquired with the property to be used as an air station. A barn or shed was sometimes turned into a hangar and a cottage became an administration building, as at the Grand Rapids (Michigan) Airport (*opposite*). Before World War I, aviation enthusiasts predicted that the delivery of freight would prove one of the most enduring purposes of flight. Far from the delivery of securities and gold and the carrying of perishable tropical goods that those prognosticators foresaw, the first "air truck" delivery (1927) was a consignment of typewriters flown from Savannah, Georgia, to Orlando, Florida. *Top:* The first United Air Express merchandise from Los Angeles, California, arrives in Tucson, Arizona, in a Fokker monoplane, 1928. *Above:* The first "terminals" in America looked very much like small railroad stations. This one served passengers on the Detroit-Cleveland Airline in the late '20s.

1925 June ... first commercial flight to Nome from Fairbanks Fokker F.III plane Pilot Noel Wien

Although Europe offered sophisticated passenger service almost immediately after World War I, American passenger operations developed as a sideline of successful mail routes. After private airlines began in 1926 to operate mail services under contract to the Post Office, passengers began to be carried regularly as part of the "cargo." One exception to this general pattern was the establishment in 1925 of passenger flights between Nome and Fairbanks, Alaska (*opposite*). Wien Alaska Airways offered services and maintained airfields that at the time would have been considered advanced in any large city in North America.

Right: Although America was far behind Europe in the development of airports, it did pioneer in night flying, an innovation that helped make aviation acceptable to businessmen who realized no saving in time by traveling only in daylight. A welcome sight to early commercial pilots, therefore, were revolving beacons which marked the way between cities on their route. This one (1927) was on the St. Louis-Chicago route of Robertson Aircraft Corp., a predecessor of what is now American Airlines. *Below:* Seven years after the governments of Europe established their first international airports, America finally had an airport of its own worthy of the name. But it took a capitalist's money to create it. Henry Ford opened his airport at Dearborn, Michigan, in 1926, the same year that his company's Tri-motor made the first flight over the North Pole.

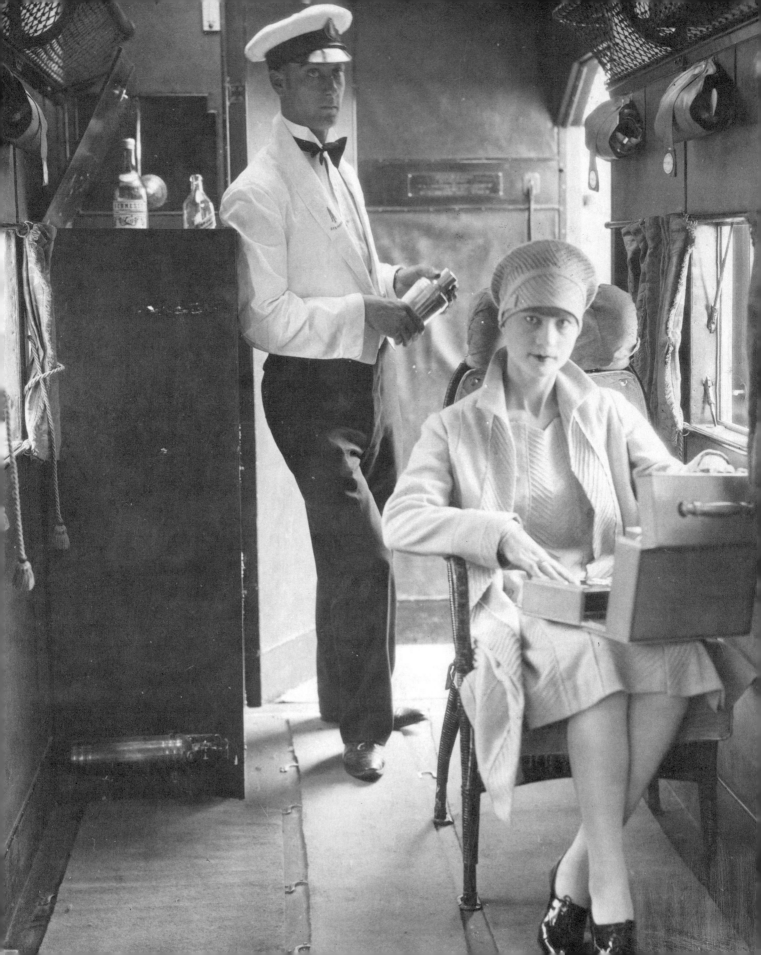

3
Le Bourget, Croydon, and Tempelhof: The First International Airports

Comparing European and American commercial air transportation during the 1920s reveals one fundamental difference: Nearly all air transport routes in Europe had been aided by direct financial subsidies from their respective governments after World War I, while such was not the case in the ruggedly individualistic America of Warren G. Harding and Calvin Coolidge. The result was that Europe offered international passenger flights of sophistication and comfort, while America remained in the Stone Age of aviation. Direct subsidies had as their primary motives the assurance of well-trained pilots, satisfactory airports, emergency landing fields, a healthy aircraft construction industry, and other features of obvious value to any nation in time of war. But the subsidy method also enabled the air transport compa-

nies in Europe to forge ahead rapidly in peacetime, establishing them well in advance of America in respect to passenger routes. That situation provided Europe with experience in the management of airports and developed facilities essential for handling international commerce. Le Bourget in Paris, Tempelhof in Berlin, Croydon in London, Schiphol in Amersterdam, Waalhaven in Rotterdam, Statens Lufthavn in Copenhagen, Littorio in Rome, and Taliedo in Milan were just some of the thriving international air terminals in Europe at a time when there wasn't a single airport worthy of the name in the entire United States.

Of all the European airports in the late '20s, the most celebrated as well as the most important were those at Le Bourget, a few miles outside Paris; at Croydon, a suburb of

Opposite: Imperial Airlines' "Silver Wing" service between London and Paris, 1927.

57

London; and at Tempelhof, some three miles from the heart of Berlin. At the time, Le Bourget and Croydon surpassed Tempelhof in world fame for two reasons: they were the termini of the best known of all aerial routes —that between Paris and London—and their names were flashed all over the world after Lindbergh landed at Le Bourget and then visited Croydon in 1927. What Tempelhof lacked in '20s "glamor," however, it more than made up for by being the busiest airport in the world. Since German commercial aviation had been developed to a degree unequalled elsewhere, Tempelhof became the center of a great aerial network that spread out from Berlin in all directions over Europe.

A contemporary description of Le Bourget in 1926 goes far in explaining why the eyes of American aviation enthusiasts were constantly on Europe while their feet were still mired in the mud of local landing fields:

> The "contrôle" at le Bourget, comparable to the office of a railroad station-master, supervises the arrival and departure of all planes. And there is a meteorological station which receives weather-reports by telephone, telegraph, and radio, and places upon large maps various cabalistic markings that enable a pilot to see at a glance the state of wind, visibility, and moisture on any European air route.
>
> On a board near the passengers' waiting-room the departures and arrivals for the day are listed, giving the hour for outgoing planes and the expected time of arrival of incoming ones. In the afternoon planes will arrive from Lyons, Cologne, Strasbourg, Vienna, London. The Cologne plane will doubtless bring passengers who transferred at Cologne from planes that had brought them from Berlin and Moscow, and the Strasbourg plane

may carry passengers who departed the day before from Warsaw, Budapest, Bucharest, or Constantinople. Other planes arriving at and departing from Le Bourget provide aerial services to Geneva, Marseille, Algeria, Spain, Morocco, and Dakar.

In a two-story building in the center of the line of hangars are the customs office, police station, and a good restaurant. Close at hand is another building containing a waiting-room, post-office, and telephones. On the second floor are the offices of the director of the airport and his staff. There is a central heating system for the hangars, a garage, oil and gasoline reservoirs, wireless station and an emergency electrical plant for lighting buildings and field, a medical establishment and a series of small buildings with offices for the flying companies, and reception-rooms for their patrons.

Extensive precautions have been taken at Le Bourget to insure the safety of passengers. A large light, much like a seacoast lighthouse, about ninety feet high, stands near the northeast extremity of the airdrome. It is lighted at sundown and is extinguished four hours later, unless a plane is expected at a later hour, when the light is kept going until the plane arrives or news is received of its arrival elsewhere. The rays of the light, which can be seen on clear nights for forty miles, flash in optical Morse signals the letter N, the code designated for Le Bourget. An acetylene light nearby is kept charged for use in case the principal one should fail. The roofs of all the hangars and other buildings are marked with red lights, and the antenna of the wireless as well as nearby factory chimneys are indicated by vertical strings of electric lamps.

A vane in the form of a white T on a black background, lighted at night, shows the aviators the direction of the wind. A pilot arriving at night drops a green rocket from a height of about 900 feet. If the way is clear, a green light is flashed from near the "contrôle" and the projectors illuminating the landing-field are turned on.

For those who could afford it, international flying was both a luxury and a convenience. Through mutual cooperation, all the governments in Europe facilitated the examination of passengers and their luggage at the ports of entry so that there was practically no delay in travel once the airport bus arrived at the terminal from the city. As one American tourist put it in 1929: "There is no rude awakening in the night or very early in the morning hours for the inspection of passports and luggage as is the case on international trains as they cross every frontier. This one feature is satisfaction enough to attract travel by air after both methods have been tried." And then there was the matter of comfort itself. The very wide concrete aprons in front of the arrival and departure buildings in Europe eliminated nearly all of the disagreeable blasts of dust and cinders that proved so annoying to passengers when airplanes started at most American landing fields. The concrete aprons also made it unnecessary for passengers to walk in mud to enter or leave the airplane. Wet and muddy shoes worn for several hours in an American airplane during cold weather were enough to discourage a passenger from ever traveling again by air.

Croydon Aerodrome took the lead in developing two-way radio communication with airplanes while in flight, so that in a fog the pilot could be told his position from radio direction—an advance quickly adopted by Le Bourget and Tempelhof—and it pioneered in procedures that made departures less nerve-jarring for early air-passengers. "At Croydon," one tourist reported, "an airplane scheduled to depart has its motors thoroughly warmed at some distance from the administration building; it is then towed by a motor tractor to its position close to the passenger terminal; the motors are started again a few minutes before the departure hour and allowed to idle quietly. There is no shouting or waving of flags or other disturbance of the passengers. When the scheduled departure minute has arrived, the control officer in the tower merely directs a beam of light toward the pilot if the field is clear for him to taxi out to the starting point." Once aboard, as the picture on p. 56 shows, the international traveler could be treated to a good stiff drink.

Although America initiated international air-travel in 1920 when Aeromarine West Indies Airways carried passengers regularly between Key West and Havana, another nine years were to pass before an American international airport—the Pan American Airways terminal in Miami—could rival European efficiency and luxury. But immediately thereafter, the Depression, for a time at least, put an end to the pursuit of luxury as an end in itself.

To mark the Paris International Exhibition of 1937, the French rebuilt Le Bourget Aerogare as a monument to modernity. The three-story terminal featured solid panes of glass extending from floor to ceiling in all rooms. Each floor was set back to provide terraces on which people could dine and enjoy the view. The roof accommodated 3000 spectators.

The "departure platform" at Croydon. The original caption of this 1929 photograph reads: "This photograph, taken from the exit traversed by all air passengers embarking at Croydon Aerodrome, shows the tranquil conditions on which an air trip from London is begun, by contrast to the turmoil of a big railway terminus."

Opposite: The original Tempelhof in 1930. Compare this outdoor public gathering place with the Chicago airport restaurant of the same period on p. 87. *Below:* The photograph is relatively modern, but the main approach to Berlin's "new" Tempelhof still looks much as it did when it was designed by National Socialists in the late 1930s to be years ahead of its time. The enormous terminal building featured a waiting room 330 feet by 160 feet, restaurants to serve 60,000 people, and a mile-long stretch of hangars under one cantilevered roof (*above*) under which 300 planes could be boarded. Over 100,000 people could watch the airport activities from the hangar roof.

Below: Haren Airport in Brussels had its modest beginnings as Belgium recovered from the devastation of World War I. This 1923 photograph illustrates the motor service that was provided city passengers by the national airline.

Above: The shed on the left was replaced a year or two later by the new Haren Airport. This 1926 photograph wonderfully captures the excitement that was once synonymous with aviation. Note the beacon, like a ship's lantern, atop the observation tower.

Opening day at Sweden's Göteborg Airport, 1923.

In 1929 an American tourist reported that "nearly all the larger European airports have designed their buildings of pleasing architecture and give the impression that commercial aviation has passed the experimental stage and has come to stay." To see just how backwards America was, compare Göteborg Airport (*above*) with Atlanta Airport (p. 12), opened two years later in 1925. The tower and passenger shed in the foreground were succeeded by a new passenger terminal in 1940 (*inset*).

The first American "international" airport of any stature was Miami's 116-acre Pan American Field, seen here on opening day in 1929. Accommodating passengers on regular flights to Havana, the terminal was rather grand for its time, since seven years would elapse before it could boast even 50 passengers a day.

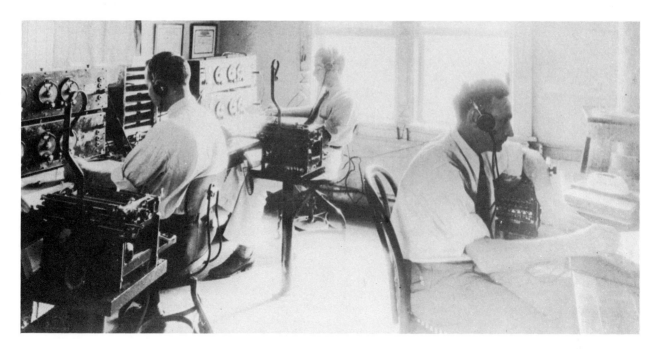

Above: An Eastern Air Transport Kingbird at Miami, 1934. The company that became Eastern Airlines moved to Pan American Field after Pan American Airways opened its new Dinner Key facilities in the same year (see pp. 142-43). Note the portable covered gangway that leads from the terminal to the plane.

Top: Radio station at Pan American Field, c. 1930. Before the perfection of the radiotelephone that permitted voice communication from plane to plane and from plane to ground, radio signals as an aid to safety in flight were sent and received by Morse code.

Left: A small Sikorsky S-38 amphibian was the plane used when Pan American Airways initiated its twice-daily flights from Miami to Cuba via Key West in 1929. Although the plane became associated with Latin America because of its use in the 1933 film *Flying Down to Rio,* it was widely popular. The passengers in this 1930 photograph are boarding at United Airport in Burbank, California. *Above:* The Fokker plane used in the early '30s by K.L.M. on the "world's longest airline," operating between Amsterdam and Java. The 8900-mile flight, originating at Schiphol Airport, took from 10 to 12 days.

A rendering of the first-prize design in the Lehigh
Airports Competition. Note the use of retractable steel
loading canopies that permit the maneuvering of
airplanes under their own power while the "tunnels" are
retracted.

4
Looking to the Future: The Architectural Competition of 1927-29

In 1927, three remarkable, but uniquely disparate, events occurred, linked solely by their place in the history of aviation: In May, Charles Lindbergh made his solo flight across the Atlantic; in September, Will Rogers published his incomparably-titled *There's Not A Bathing Suit in Russia,* lambasting America for lagging behind the rest of the world in commercial aviation; and, at the end of the year, the Lehigh Portland Cement Company of Allentown, Pennsylvania, announced the world's first architectural competition for the design of "modern airports." The Lindbergh story immediately transcended mere history and became the stuff of heroic legend, an act of courage that has lost little of its elemental power after more than half a century. The fame of Will Rogers, on the other hand, rests almost entirely on his career in show business. If few remember the Oklahoman as a pioneering proponent of aviation, angered by America's footdragging in the development of air terminals ("Nobody is walking but us; Everybody else is flying"), then no one, rest assured, remembers the Lehigh Airports Competition. Yet, when the award-winning designs were announced in 1929, and published in 1930, they received world-wide acclaim and seemed to promise both an answer to Rogers' criticism and fulfillment of Lindbergh's prophecy: "Large and well-equipped airports . . . will place the United States at the top in aeronautical activity." The designs on the following pages, published through the courtesy of the Lehigh Portland Cement Company, have not been seen in fifty years.

The first-prize design of A. C. Zimmerman and W. H. Harrison featured a quadrant-shaped field providing 16 take-off directions. Passengers were to proceed from the main terminal by tunnel to a star-shaped boarding area.

Fourth-prize winner W. R. Amon envisioned a circular
flying field, direct access from a public plaza to the
terminal building, and covered loading decks. But he was
faulted for locating some buildings across the ends of
runways.

The design of C. A. Stone and U. F. Rible was praised for its "very interesting architectural treatment," but criticized for its unusually wide apron completely encircling the field and for the two runways heading directly for the crowd of people seated in the stadium!

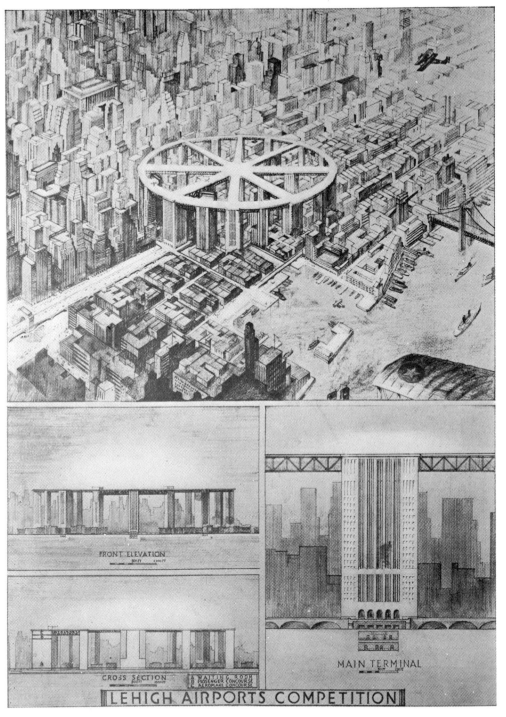

H. Altvater's "visionary scheme," the judges wrote, reflected "originality rather than any elements of practical utility." An airport similar to this "huge wheel resting on the roofs of many skyscrapers" was actually planned for London (p. 130).

The judges praised the "modernistic" design of J. L.
Cannon's terminal building and its covered loading bays
and overhead observation roof. What they termed
"modernistic" is now erroneously called Art Déco.

LEHIGH · AIRPORTS · COMPETITION

In this design by Britton Kirton, the hangar roofs constitute an observation platform allowing "convenient and safe public view of airport activities." "The tower," said the judges, "is exceedingly dangerous and quite unnecessary."

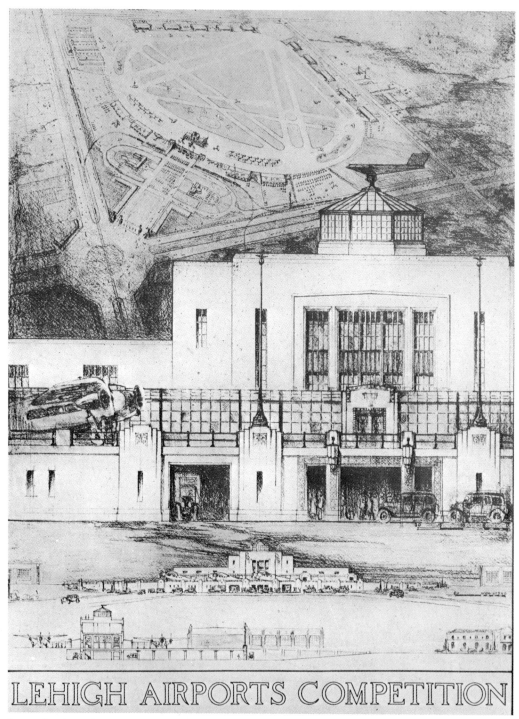

LEHIGH AIRPORTS COMPETITION

Appearing in architectural style very much like New York's East Side Airlines Terminal built ten years later, R. H. MacNaughton's design provided the unlikely feature of passenger planes loading directly at the terminal's front door.

LEHIGH AIRPORTS COMPETITION

The design of T. H. Locraft and R. C. Danis envisioned overhead passageways connecting the terminal with the principal hangars and with the covered landing bays that are projected well out into the field. Flash Gordon would have loved it.

Terminal for ocean liners, trains, airplanes, and
seaplanes, designed in 1928 by The Austin Company.

5
The Airport as Railroad Terminal: Flying in the '20s and '30s

"All Aboard for the Twentieth-Century Flyer." So ran the headline of an article in *The Literary Digest* that greeted credulous readers eager for aviation news shortly after Lindbergh's historic flight in 1927. "Passengers have been weighed," the article declared, "and so have their bags, and now they wait on the concrete-covered area of the airport, just as one waits on a railway station or a steamboat landing. In fact, there is the same activity of brass-buttoned officials and porters with their hand trucks. One is about to take a journey, and the atmosphere is appropriate to embarkation. . . . Aha! Here she comes! With a roar from its great motors a gigantic biplane pulls up to the edge of the concrete. Its pilot, who sits in a small cockpit at the very nose of the plane, climbs down for a final look at his machine. A white-jacketed steward opens the door of the car. Twenty wicker chairs are revealed, arranged like the seats in a commuter railway-car, each at a window, with an aisle down the middle. The passengers enter. The hand baggage and mail are stuffed into the 'hold.' There is a whir from the motors, the chocks are removed from before the rubber-tired wheels and the ship begins to move. And so, 'we're off,' with something more than the emotional thrill belonging to a start for Chicago on the *Twentieth Century Limited*. For 'we're off' from Le Bourget to Croydon—from Paris to London—by way of the air. And, some day soon, from New York to London or from Boston to Berlin."

That air travel could be likened by enthusiasts to the ease and comfort of the railroad was hardly surprising, for, by the late

'20s, almost everyone realized that commercial aviation would grow only when passengers were freed from muddy landing fields and the hazard of whirring propellers. And almost everyone foresaw that the "air depot" of the future would have to follow closely the methods of modern railroad terminals if aviation were to prove more than a fad, a sport, or a novel way to move the mails. "Terminals, similar to those operated by railroads," an engineering magazine announced in 1929, "are being planned to provide comfort, safety, and convenience for air-travelers, who are now in many cases compelled to land in open fields. In the near future we will have passenger facilities at airports that will compete with those now to be found in the terminal stations of important railway lines." Air depots of the future were to "follow closely the methods of modern railroad terminals," in much the same manner as the airport pictured on p. 82. Passengers were to go through the airport to concourses that would take them to waiting planes, which they could enter without leaving cover. Such air stations would consist of "artistically designed" two-story building units connected by steel bridges which would serve as concourses, the buildings themselves serving as piers for the spans of covered concourse bridges. The space beneath the spans and between the piers would form covered loading areas for the planes. As a passenger arrived at the terminal, he would enter the waiting room under a marquee at the entrance, purchase his ticket, and go to the passenger concourse on the mezzanine floor. When the plane was announced, he would descend a stairway built in one of the piers and walk across a portable railed-in passageway, similar to a ship's gangplank, and through the open door of the plane directly to his seat. These portable passage-ways, of course, were the forerunners of the covered boarding gangways leading to today's jumbo jets. A variation of this plan was to have a passageway in the form of subways underground instead of building overhead bridges (see pp. 88-89).

The notion of the airport as a railroad terminal for air passengers was an architectural commonplace by the late '20s and is apparent not only in many of the illustrations that follow, but in the prize-winning entries of the Lehigh Airports Competition as well. The idea was recommended in technical periodicals ("Airports should resemble large railroad terminals," reported *Iron Age* in 1929), trumpeted in the popular press ("The airport depot of the future," wrote *The Literary Digest* in the same year, "will be like the terminal stations of important railway lines today"), and declaimed in full-length books ("The airport is like a railroad station," wrote Stedman Hanks in *International Airports* [1929]). But in applying the idea beyond the level of superficial architectural form, few were as clearheaded as a city planner named John Nolen, who, in a 1928 pamphlet entitled *Airports and Airways,* saw how the development of commercial aviation could benefit from the experience of railroading. As early as World War I, flying enthusiasts had complained about the location of landing fields on the outskirts of the city and wanted these facilities placed closer to town or even within the city itself. "Should airports be as central as possible, or on the outskirts?" asked Nolen:

> In earlier days, when the railroad was in its pioneer stages, the aim was to get a central situation in a city for its stations or terminal. In more recent times it has often been found that it would be better on the whole to be farther from the center of the city. What is true of the rail-

road stations is true of other semi-public buildings and municipal buildings. All have a tendency to move out. The principle of decentralization is being more and more widely applied. The reasons are: First, the increasing congestion of the built up sections of cities; second, the desire to get rid of noise and other nuisances; and, finally, the new means now available in the motor vehicle for convenient supplementary, closely related transportation service.

Another railroad policy which could be considered with profit is that of the union depot idea, a single station for a number of railroads, or for all of the railroads entering a city. The advantages need to be considered, pro and con, of a single station as compared with a number of well-distributed stations. Applied to air travel, the question might be raised of the advantages of one or more landing fields in a large city or metropolitan region at which aircraft would be served, as against separate ports or landing fields for airplanes, for airships, for balloons, and for seaplanes.

Another point for profitable reflection is that of the correlation of different forms of transportation —rail, road, and water. Consideration should be given early in the location of airports to this correlation by the linking of the air service with other forms of transportation. The main point is that planning for aircraft should be related, coordinated planning. After all, airports and landing fields are merely terminals or stations or transfer points in a larger transportation system.

More than half a century later, the last of John Nolen's "reflections" is still far from successful resolution, but the first two—those related to railroading—are long-accepted realities. By 1939 the union-terminal idea was virtually universal, and only those who had never heard of the DC-3s and Boeing Stratoliners, streamlined giants that held 36 passengers, still dreamed of center-city airports. Ironically, these very same "supertransports" of the late '30s immediately outdated every airport built in the preceding decade and brought to a close the era of the airport as railroad terminal. A war would soon bring about the development of jet propulsion and the eventual growth of airports as small cities in themselves.

The Universal Air Lines passenger station in Chicago is typical of American terminals in the late '20s. Most airlines provided transportation to the landing field from offices in town (*left*).

Opposite: Waiting rooms, generally cheerless, were frequently decorated with wicker furniture, suggesting the lightweight wicker seats to be found on passenger planes. Note the scale in the background used for weighing passengers before boarding. Airport restaurants were no less gruesome than the hash-houses that passed for railroad-station lunchrooms throughout America. The palm tree is a masterful decorating touch for chilly Chicago.

Central Airport in Camden, New Jersey, announces its opening in 1929: "In addition to enormous hangars are weather services, radio, complete lighting for night flying, a splendid restaurant, two swimming pools with a sand beach, and parking for 4000 cars." Without federal assistance, airports had to attract paying spectators to survive.

PHILADELPHIA-CAMDEN

CENTRAL AIRPORT

In Wilbert J. Austin's design for a combined train and air terminal (1928), the safety of passengers and their protection from the elements are assured by means of an underground tunnel to "ship stations."

The Austin Company designed and built some of the first large airports in America. Since cities throughout the country were planning municipal fields, Austin advertised its expertise with renderings like the one above (c. 1928).

Air transportation had scarcely begun in the United States before it was realized that real public acceptance of its services could only be forthcoming if the airlines could operate as much by night as by day. Since the majority of travelers were (and are) business people, time in transit was measured not so much in terms of absolute hours as in business hours. Even though night flying was proved practical in the late '20s, the airlines believed that most travelers would be too frightened to fly after dark. Consequently, in 1929, Trans World Airlines (then known as Transcontinental Air Transport), in cooperation with the Pennsylvania and the Santa Fe Railroads, organized an "Air-Rail" service whereby passengers flew by day and then were transferred to railroad sleeping cars during the hours of darkness. Two nights aboard sleeping cars and two days aboard TAT planes were required for the transcontinental run. The coast-to-coast service was discontinued a few years later when as many air travelers began to fly by night as by day. *Above:* An exhibit promoting the Air-Rail service in New York's Pennsylvania Station. The presence of an airplane in the now-demolished station is eerily prophetic. *Opposite, above:* The maiden run of *The Airway Limited* on the first leg of the transcontinental trip. On board were Col. and Mrs. Charles A. Lindbergh and Amelia Earhart. *Opposite:* Boarding a Ford Trimotor the following morning at Columbus, Ohio.

Night flying came as a result of an effort to improve the efficiency of air mail. As early as 1923, the Post Office established an experimental lighted airway on the route between Chicago and Cheyenne. Regular night mail service was begun in 1924, was extended to New York the following year, and before the end of 1926 the airway from New York to San Francisco was completely equipped for night operations. Through the 1920s and '30s technicians developed and improved such lighting devices for safe nocturnal flights as revolving beacons, illuminated wind-direction indicators, boundary lights, approach lights, runway contact lights, obstruction lights, and a complete landing-area floodlight system. *Above:* The tower at the Omaha (Nebraska) Municipal Airport (1930) was typical of revolving beacons that were visible for miles and informed flyers that an airfield was available. *Opposite, center:* Airplanes at Felts Field, Spokane, Washington, in 1927.

While architects dreamed of air terminals that, like the great railroad stations of the day, provided protection from the elements for weary travelers, most air passengers in the late '20s and early '30s were forced to wade through puddles or to make their way through dirt and dust while boarding planes. The scene at an airfield in Grand Rapids, Michigan (*opposite, top*), is typical of the period. Passengers seemed an afterthought to freight. *Opposite, below:* No one doubts that the eventual success of air-mail service led both to improved landing fields and to increased passenger service. The photograph of the Pitcairn Airways hangar at Miami Municipal Airport (c. 1928) suggests the link between air mail and passenger service in America. When Eddie Rickenbacker's Florida Airways failed to show a profit by flying the mails in the early 1920s, his business was purchased by Harold Pitcairn. Pitcairn's profitable operations eventually became Eastern Airlines.

The Kansas City (Missouri) Municipal Airport was dedicated by Charles Lindbergh in 1927 when he was acting as an advisor to Transcontinental Air Transport—then known as the "Lindbergh Line"—in the selection of airport sites. Lindbergh was so impressed by Kansas City's interest in aviation that TAT (later TWA) chose the city as its corporate headquarters. This 1929 photograph shows a TAT Ford Tri-motor aptly named *The Kansas City.*

Seen against a backdrop of the 1933 National Air Races
at Mines Field (Los Angeles Municipal Airport) is Hangar
#1, built for the Curtiss-Wright Company in 1929. This
Spanish Colonial building was actually two separate
hangars connected by an administrative building topped
by a decorative tower. It was not a control tower since all
air traffic was directed from the ground with the use of
flags.

The waiting room of the Cheyenne (Wyoming) Municipal Airport in 1928 is typical of passenger facilities at smaller American flying fields during the early days of commercial aviation. The widely spaced wicker furniture was ample for the few passengers carried or for those who awaited them. A radio receiver at the far end provided entertainment.

Opposite, top: The Tacoma (Washington) Airport in 1927 presents an architectural design typical of the '20s and '30s—a single wide-span hangar with a one- or two-story shed attached for both administrative offices and a waiting room. The waiting room would very likely have been similar to the one in Cheyenne. *Opposite:* By the close of the 1920s, Bowman Field had grown from the cornfield on p. 24 to the complex of hangars and buildings shown here.

Newark (New Jersey) Airport in 1929. The Ford Tri-motor (*below*) was one of the principal airlines in service and easily fit into the large hangar at the rear. The original tower and a bank of ramp lights are behind the aircraft. For several years air travelers and visitors could drive right up to the landing areas *(left)*.

Left: A Sikorsky S-38 prepares for take-off at Dinner Key, Miami, Florida, in 1931. Three years later Pan American Airways replaced its rickety pier-like seaplane port with a new terminal (pp. 112-13).

Against a backdrop of original architectural elevations outlining the Spanish Colonial styling then considered *de rigueur* for public buildings in the Southwest is seen Burbank, California's United Airport shortly after it opened in 1930. Hailed as the nation's most modern airport, United boasted a new form of cushioned runway, developed by Boeing and Standard Oil, that became an industry standard for many years.

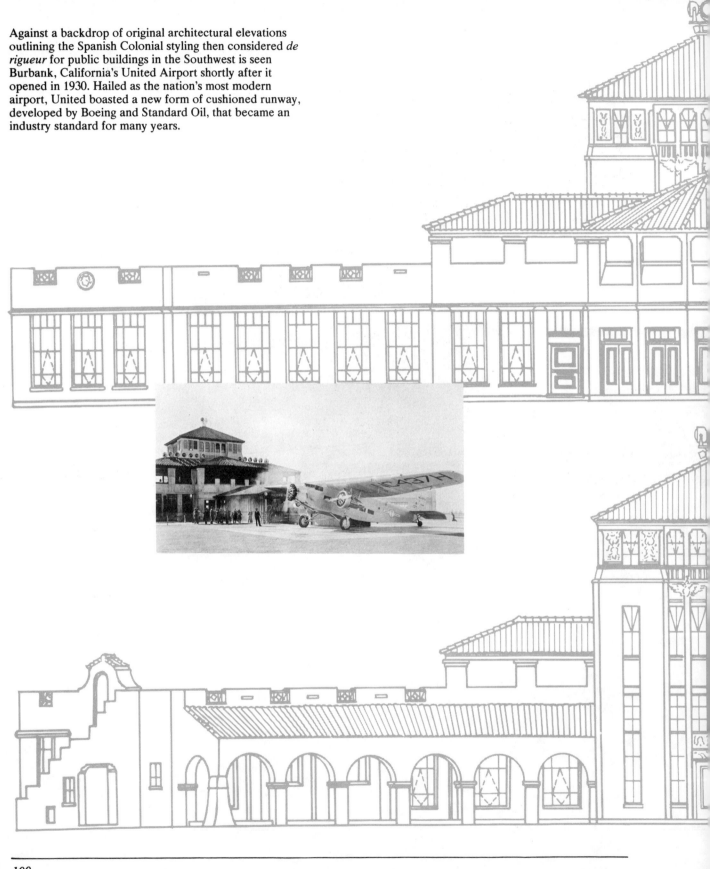

United Airport's impressive interiors were remarkably similar to those of the nearby Los Angeles Union Railroad Terminal, built nine years later. Both were "modernistic" treatments of Spanish themes. As modern as this airport was in its day, its first wind indicator was unusually primitive—a smoke pot, much like those used in California orange groves, sunk in a pit at the intersection of the runways.

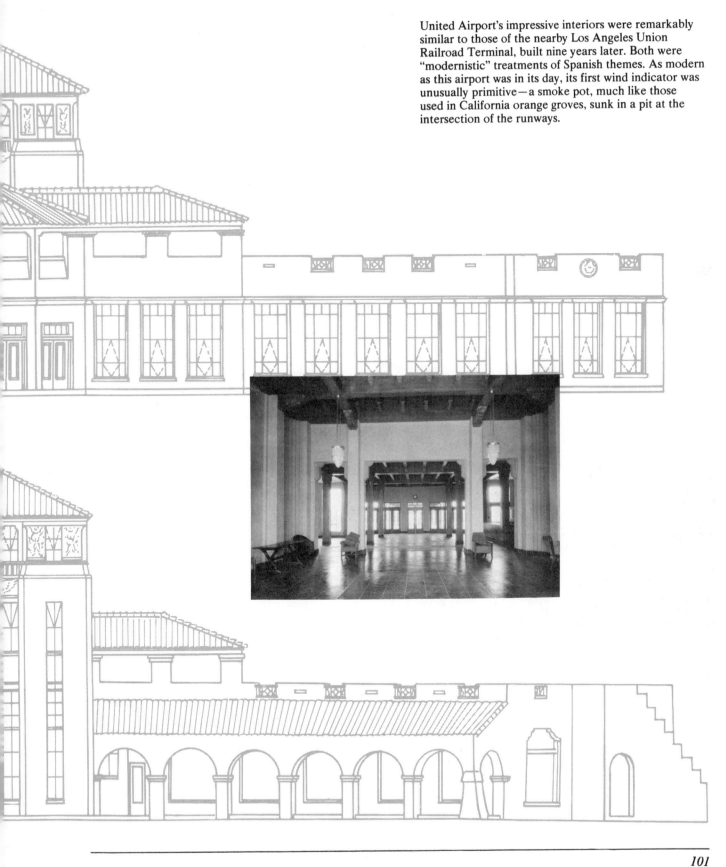

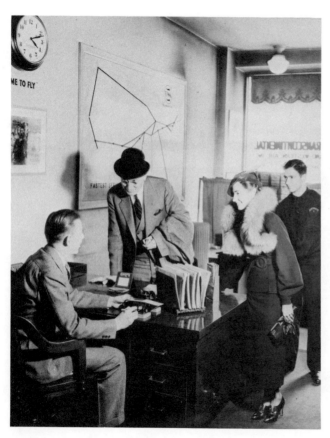

Early in 1930, an American journalist, eager to impress upon his readers the importance of the airport in the coming air age, and the excitement of air travel, wrote the following: "Rail and highway transportation are confined in a broad sense to one dimension, along the line of the rails or the road; water transportation operates, generally speaking, in two dimensions, the plane of the navigable body of water; but air transportation has a sphere of operation in three dimensions—space. The domain of aircraft being limited only by man's mechanical ability and his endurance, the airports, or places of beginning and ending air journeys, may truly be called portals to the sky. Railroad and dock stations are to most people simply places to get on or off trains and boats. But the requirements of transportation demand elaborate equipment and personnel hardly known to the average person, at these centers of arrival and departure. Similarly, the airport is more than a landing field. In addition to facilities for receiving and discharging passengers or cargo by air, it must be equipped to shelter, supply and repair aircraft, to guide planes safely to earth in darkness and storm, to supply weather reports to flyers, to sort and stamp air mail, to give rest and food to weary pilots and mechanics, and to meet sudden emergencies of fire and accident."

A few of the many activities associated with flying in the early days of the Great Depression are seen on these pages. Long before telephones played Muzak while one waited for an airlines reservation clerk, passengers made their reservations at such computerless sales offices as the TAT office in St. Louis (*left*). The clock on the wall reminds the passengers that "It's Time To Fly." *Opposite, top:* Passengers could also purchase their tickets directly at the airport, as this photograph of the United Airlines waiting room in Dallas, Texas, shows. At the time (1931), several movie theaters in Dallas had bigger lobbies and box offices. *Center:* An aviator checks weather conditions at his destination after a report has been received by Teletype. *Below:* Ground attendants load baggage in the bin-like hold within the wing of a Tri-motor.

All the excitement of early aviation as a spectator event is contained in this photograph (*above*) of crowds attending an air meet at the Wayne County (Michigan) Airport in 1935. Note the hundreds of spectators on the tiered roof. Throughout the 1920s, when the American air transportation industry had not yet realized a profit, and into the '30s, when profits were marginal, airports were urged to sponsor public events and to develop their concessions to defray operating expenses. The Wayne County Airport was actually a large hangar with administration and passenger facilities, a plan less pretentiously realized (*below*) in the headquarters of Kansas City's National Air Transport (a predecessor of United Airlines). The hangar has an Austin cantilevered canopy door.

Opposite: So many American airports were merely hangars with small administration wings attached that experienced travelers, used to the relative luxury of Schiphol, Le Bourget, and other European terminals, complained that "too many of our air depots resemble factory buildings rather than passenger terminals." Architectural treatment is very frequently related to the question of money, and even the judges of the Lehigh Airports Competition despaired that taxpayers would ever permit construction of the best designs. Still, there were exceptions in America, and the modernistic Swan Island Airport in Portland, Oregon (1930), was one of them.

Left: Wichita (Kansas) Airport as it appeared in March, 1938, on the occasion of the first visit of the giant DC-3s that outmoded most airfields. The Airport opened in 1929 and operated from the Air Capitol hangar-terminal (in the background) until the administration building (*above*), delayed by the Depression, finally opened in 1935. When their flight was announced, passengers in the waiting room (*above*) would descend to the airfield loading ramp. From 1929 until the advent of superliners, aircraft landed on sod runways. Well-drained flint-rock topsoil permitted all-weather operation, and beacon lights made night flying possible.

Chicago Municipal Airport (later Midway) as it appeared in the mid-'30s. A canopy from the gate to the airfield protected passengers from the elements.

America's most famous elected officials arrived at and departed from this terminal building during the Depression years. Washington Airport installed the nation's first radio control tower and dispensed with the use of signal flags in 1934.

Iowa City Municipal Airport illuminated for a night landing in the early 1930s. The rotating beacon could be seen for miles by the approaching pilot before he put down, aided by the airport floodlights.

This view of the Pontiac (Michigan) Municipal Airport in the early '30s is of interest because of its close-up view of a field boundary light mounted on a colored day marker cone.

In the depth of the Depression, when construction work
of all kinds was at its lowest ebb, and when the few large
projects were frequently built in the dull WPA civic style,
The Austin Company of Cleveland, Ohio, launched an
advertising campaign in *Fortune* magazine that featured
prototypical architectural models. Among these "dream
concepts" were several airports, all designed by architect
Robert Smith. The strange airplane-shaped terminal
(*above*) is actually a long hangar that can be entered
from two sides, crowned by two cantilevered "wings"
providing shelter, and joined by a four-story
administration building-passenger hall-control tower.
Opposite: The "Inter-Continental Airways" terminal is a
Depression Modern variation on the old hangar-
passenger shed theme, worthy of *Things to Come.* The
seaplane base, inspired by Pan Am's Flying Clippers,
features a luxury hotel.

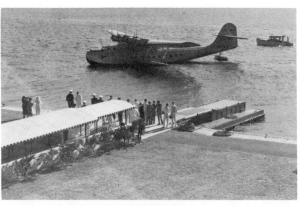

The new seaplane terminal that Pan American Airways opened in 1934 at Dinner Key, Miami, was one of the first American airports to be touted in the world's architectural magazines. Its facilities were perfectly matched to the needs of passengers on Pan Am's Clippers, the epitome of luxury-airliners during the Depression.

A superliner that outmoded airports worldwide.

Tourists only—since the big birds couldn't land most places.

The grass at Fargo, North Dakota, would have to go.

The axiom holds: the aircraft predicates the airport.

Albuquerque Municipal Airport, opened in 1939, was a WPA project in steel and adobe designed by E. H. Blumenthal who adapted New Mexico's Pueblo Revival style of architecture to the requirements of air traffic. The building's long, low lines are broken by the control tower, "a successful combination of local tradition and technical necessities." The waiting room, with its carved rafters and flagstone floors, resembles railroad stations built in the same manner. This outstanding structure has been preserved and is now the home of the Museum of Albuquerque.

When New York Municipal Airport (later La Guardia)
was built for the 1939 World's Fair, it was considered the
most modern in America. Designed by the firm of Delano
& Aldrich for the WPA, the structure—from the circular
ramp to the ribbon-strip windows and the stainless-steel
eagle named "The Spirit of Flight"—is a model of
Depression architecture.

Dining at the glass-enclosed Sky Lounge at La Guardia in
1939. Ten years earlier, an American dining at Le
Bourget Aèrogare had noted that "visitors who
remain in comfortable restaurants while observing
airplanes as they alight and depart are certain to become
patrons of air transportation lines." Note the promenade
from which thousands of spectators could observe the
field.

The '30s ended with the oncoming clouds of war and the
expansion of runways to accommodate heavier aircraft.
Counterclockwise: the municipal airports of Kansas City,
Missouri; Houston, Texas; and Buffalo, New York, in
1939.

The amazing feats of early aviators led to some equally amazing visions by earthbound dreamers. This cut appeared in a conservative business magazine in 1929.

6
Dreams and Visions: Seadromes, Mooring Masts, and Skyports

The history of aviation is in many ways the story of dreamers and their dreams. One of the most persistent of these dreams, one that waited half a century to become a practical reality, was the idea of commercial transatlantic flight. If early thinkers envisioned long-distance overland flying as a series of touchdowns on airfields evenly spaced, transoceanic flight was seen as possible only if passenger planes alighted on a series of man-made islands called "seadromes." One such floating airport, the Armstrong Seadrome, was to be an enormous landing platform supported by telescopic columns extending far below the sea where there is no wave motion, no matter how tumultous the surface billows, to disturb the ballasting chambers placed in this zone of perpetual calm. Since the platform itself was to be raised out of the water, far above the highest recorded wave level, the seadrome—equipped with hotel facilities for weary travelers— would remain level and unmoved in calm and storm. This incredible idea—dating from World War I and funded by the United States in 1934—remained active on drawing boards until the late 1940s. Although critics saw transatlantic dirigibles rendering seadromes unnecessary, the *Hindenburg* disaster of 1937 revived interest in oceanic airports, just as the autogyro reawakened the idea of mid-city "skyports," some circular, some floating (as in Norman Bel Geddes' dream of a major airport in New York Bay), but none so fantastic as 1939's vision of a 200-story skyscraper for flying commuters, complete with 75 floors of hangars for convenient parking!

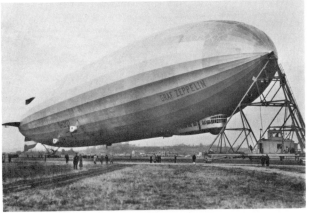

Until the tragic end of the *Hindenburg* in 1937, the one rival to the development of practical heavier-than-air transatlantic travel was the lighter-than-air dirigible. But even though airships provided successful luxury-class flight, there was the problem of how to house the aerial behemoths. *Opposite:* Shed for a small airship at Wheeling, West Virginia, 1927. Above the hangar (*right*) is the *Graf Zeppelin* tied to a portable mooring mast that will lead it to its shed, and (*left*) the British airship *R-100* at its mooring mast at Cardington, Bedfordshire. *Right:* The Ford Mooring Tower.

Left: The Ford Mooring Tower. *Top:* The Italian airship *Norge* leaves Spitzbergen for its trip over the North Pole in 1926. *Above:* The ill-fated *R-101* at its base at Cardington.

Commercial transatlantic flight was a long-unrealized dream. *Top:* A German cartoon predicts the future after Lindbergh's flight: "Daddy, what's that funny thing down there?" *Above:* A proposed floating island for ocean-going airplanes (1924).

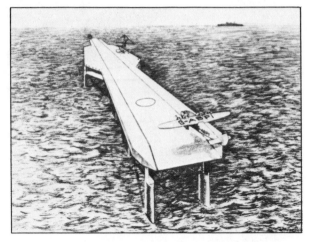

It was once believed that a chain of five Armstrong Seadromes would make Atlantic flight possible. Basically, the seadrome was a landing platform 1200 feet long and 350 feet wide, supported by streamlined, telescopic columns which extended far below the sea. Although the plan had adherents for 25 years, none was ever built. *Below:* A perspective view of a seadrome showing the immersed portion as well as that above the water. The elevator for taking planes from the landing deck to the hangar deck below is shown. *Opposite page, top:* Pilot's view of landing deck. *Center:* Deck scene showing plane elevator in foreground. *Bottom:* Lower deck, containing hangars, repair shops, dwelling quarters for the crew, and hotel accommodations for passengers.

This roof-top Croydon, proposed in 1931, called for 36
buildings at London's King's Cross to serve as pillars for a
126-acre "aerial hub."

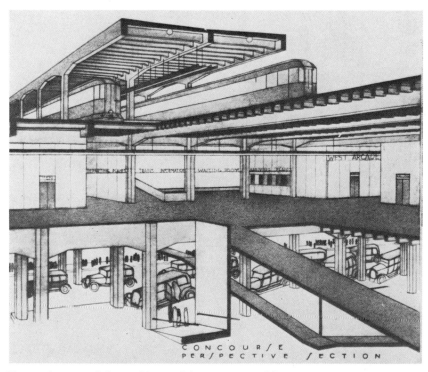

CONCOURSE
PERSPECTIVE SECTION

Foreseeing one of the problems of the present, architect
Richard Neutra proposed the idea of the airport as "a
transfer point," linked directly to other mass
transportation (1930).

Control tower, Norton Air Force Base, California.

7
The Airport Goes to War

In July, 1942, America's commercial flying schedules were reduced by half in order to furnish needed planes to the armed forces. That drastic action to further national defense had its effect on every airport in the country. Within a few days after Pearl Harbor U.S. military forces moved in almost completely on 100 of the largest and best equipped of the nation's 2,484 airports. As of January, 1944, Army and Navy operations accounted for 89.1 percent of all domestic flights, and itinerant flying took up another 3.1 percent, leaving the tiny balance for the air carriers. Most airports, however, were not immediately suitable for military operations. Runways built to stand the impact from 4,000-pound aircraft could not take the pounding of 25-ton planes, let alone the Fortresses, Liberators, and other air giants which weighed far more, even if the runways were long enough for take-offs and landings. On January 1, 1942 the United States had 187 airports capable of handling airplanes up to 50,000 pounds gross weight. By 1945 there were 430 in this class. In 1942 there were just 72 airfields adequate for plane weights of 50,000 or more, and by 1945 there were 655. That is one way to describe what was done to landing facilities during the war in order to keep pace with aerodynamics. By V-J Day it was clear that the wartime trend toward larger, faster, farther-flying aircraft would outmode terminals worldwide, and it was equally obvious that postwar plane travel, by the very magnitude of planes and the number of people who would ride in them, would demand dramatic changes in the general conception of airports.

Top: The Maxwell Air Force Base (Montgomery, Alabama) was built on the site of the Wright Brothers' 1910 flying school. In 1941 French, English, and American pilots were in training here. *Above:* A line-up of Tiger Moths at High River, Alberta, 1943. *Opposite:* Miami's Eastern Airline Terminal as a military base, 1943.

Left: 1929's United Airport in Burbank is camouflaged for the war effort in 1943. Beneath the jungle are Spanish Colonial buildings.

Above: The only passengers in the lobby of the same airport are U.S. servicemen and their families.

War-torn Europe begins to recover: London Airport in
1946. The main passenger departure lounge is in a tent.
The presence of the booksellers W. H. Smith & Son,
ubiquitous in British air and rail depots, signifies a return
to normalcy.

Battered Tempelhof was perhaps never so important as when the Berlin Airlift of 1948-49 broke through the Soviet blockade of the city by nonstop supply shipments to its 2.5 million residents.

Houston Intercontinental Airport, a jet-age terminal for a
city wedded to the internal-combustion engine.

8
Winging It in the Jet Age: The Modern Terminal

In 1926, all the airlines in the United States put together had a total of only 28 planes. If all of those planes were in the air at one time, and all their seats were occupied, there would have been 112 passengers in the air. Today, of course, a single jumbo jet carries roughly three times that number of travelers, with a potential load even greater, and the nation's fleet of 2600 commercial aircraft carries some 280 million passengers annually, a number greater than that of the total population of the country. By 1990, more than 455 million American travelers are expected to use airports and, since many passengers are seen off or welcomed back by relatives and friends, it is hardly an exaggeration to expect that in the final decade before the 21st century, over 1 billion people annually will be using the services of American airports alone. Add to this already astonishing figure the millions upon millions of Canadians, Germans, Japanese, Brazilians, Australians, and other citizens of the world who fly regularly or even occasionally—plus the people who accompany them to or from their flights—and the total number borders on the incredible.

In surveying the history of the airport, there seem to be three constants: (1) the airport is a mutable form (constantly under construction, no airport has ever called itself "complete"); (2) the "new" airport, even if hailed as "ahead of its time," is soon congested or even out of date; (3) faced with new developments in aviation technology, the airport adapts accordingly to accommodate those developments: In short, *the airplane predicates the airport,* and not the other way around. The third factor, of course, brings about the first two and has been the observable lowest common denominator of airport planning and management for well over 50 years.

A 1938 magazine article, aptly entitled "No Place to Land," complained that the introduction of the DC-3 and other large aircraft had brought about "a failure to balance aviation's tremendous technical progress with suitable landing fields." And the charge was made again and again in the '40s and '50s as postwar aeronautics produced such giants as the 92-ton double-decked Lockheed Constitution which could carry 180 passengers. The increased numbers of passengers drawn to air travel required not merely longer runways for larger aircraft, but larger, more sophisticated terminals to handle the needs of travelers—from ticketing, check-in, baggage retrieval, and restaurant facilities (the things a passenger can see) to sewerage systems, fire-fighting equipment, and radar and electronic controls (the things he can't). In the early '50s, one airport manager complained of the fundamental requirement that airport design follow aircraft technology: "No bus designer would dream of building a bus twice as wide as the average highway and expect the states and towns to go out and widen all their roads. Why can't aircraft designers design for the airport instead of the other way around?" But this cry had already been heard in 1938 and answered in World War II. The close ties of civil aviation to military aviation allowed no safe way to hold back the advance of aeronautics. With air power a key factor in national defense, the military counted heavily on the airlines for a ready reserve transport capacity in time of emergency. Airports would have to grow to suit the planes, like it or not.

And grow they did. First to accommodate the large prop planes that made transoceanic flight a commonplace by mid-century, and then to adjust to the dramatic changes brought about by the success of jet-propelled aircraft. The phenomenal popularity of jet travel—over land and sea—can be best measured in its impact on other modes of transportation. The same year (1967) which saw the disappearance of the New York Central Railroad's *Twentieth Century Limited* also saw the last voyage of the Cunard liner, the *Queen Mary.* The fast new jet airliner was responsible for the demise of both transcontinental rail travel and of transoceanic luxury liners. And with fewer trains and almost no ships at all, where was the traveler to turn—except to the crowded airport?

The first siren whoosh of the commercial jetliner in the late '50s not only changed man's notion of time and travel by shrinking the earth some 40 percent, but set off an earthbound revolution that transformed the whole façade and function of the jet-age airport. Nations and cities took a searching second look at the airports that served the piston-plane age and found them wanting. The result was a worldwide building boom to adapt or completely rebuild them to the new and challenging problems of jet transportation. In addition to building the enormous runways required for jet take-offs and landings, airports throughout the '60s changed their profiles by the addition of "jetways," "fingers," or "satellites," three of many names for the new covered corridors that telescope out from the main terminal building to meet the planes, sometimes in graceful star-shaped structures that nestle many jets at one time. Although airports learned to place ticket counters close to the entrance so that passengers could drop their heavy bags and line up to buy tickets, the new satellite areas increased the amount of walking that faced passengers before they reached their planes. To solve this new problem, some airports installed moving sidewalks, and some, like Washington's Dulles and Montreal's Mirabel, completely eliminated passageways reaching out into the apron. Instead of jets coming up to terminal "fingers," passengers in these airports simply boarded giant "mobile lounges" that moved them out to the jets. To avoid jam-ups anticipated at baggage-claim areas, airport planners installed either revolving baggage carousels or perpetual motion conveyor belts to sort and store passengers' luggage automatically.

But all this, and far more—enormous parking lots, new expressways, the development of the swinging, telescoping, covered aero-gangplank—were hardly enough. In 1959, the first full year of commercial jet travel, 51 million domestic passengers boarded planes in United States airports. Less than ten years later, in 1968, the total more than doubled to 115 million—and this was two years before such jumbo jets as the Boeing 747 and the Douglas DC-10 were adding still additional hundreds of passengers and thousands of pieces of luggage to already crowded terminals. The result was a repetition of the headlines of 1938 when critics complained that "aviation policy has given us 1926 airports for 1938 planes." This time, in 1968, the complaint, as *Time* magazine put it, was that "airports are straining at the seams." Now, more than a decade later, with such airport "cities" as Kennedy, Los Angeles International, Leonardo da Vinci, and Heathrow, having expanded still again, the cry is heard once more. This is how *The Wall Street Journal* headlined it in the summer of 1979: "Jumbo Jumble: Surge of Travelers on Big Jets Strains Capacity of Terminals at Major Airports." "The airports," the article chided, "aren't keeping up with passenger growth. They've run out of space . . . and are trying to put a quart of air travel into a pint pot."

The only consolation, it seems, is the similarity of rhetoric from age to age: In 1938 the complaint was that "we have hatched eagles for the world's airways—and provided them with wren's nests." Wren's nests or pint pots, considering how the airport has managed to evolve over the years—an evolution documented by the pictures in this book—the future seems likely to survive the shortcomings of the present, just as the present has survived the inadequacies of the past. As S. P. Cockerell wrote almost 70 years ago in the pioneering days of aviation, "Are we to believe that the ever-swelling number of men who are devoting their lives to the perfection of human flight will accept any arbitrary limitations to the scope of practical possibilities?"

Well, hardly. Noise, yes. Congestion, yes. Frustration, yes. But think of the miracle of moving a billion people and more from city to city and over mountains and seas, and marvel at how far we've come from putting down on fallow cornfields and how far we've yet to go.

Overleaf: The plan of a modern terminal: Sweden's Göteborg-Landvetter Airport.

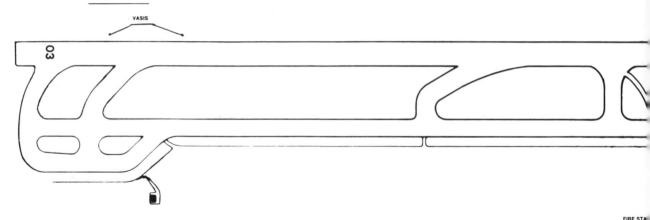

GLIDEPATH TRANSMITTER

VASIS

03

FIRE STA

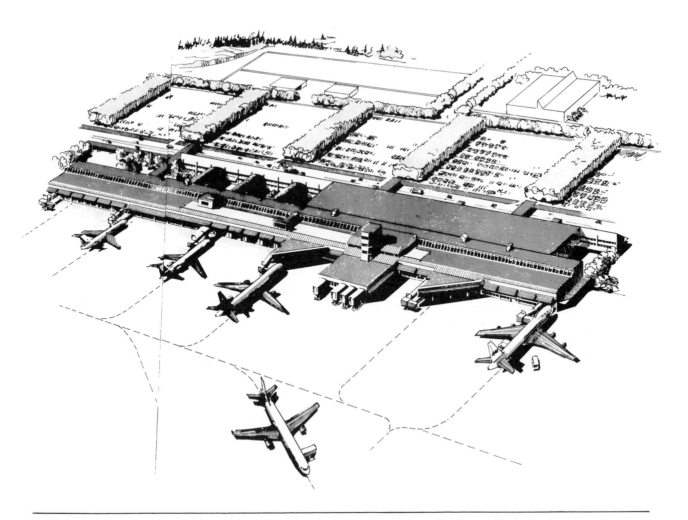

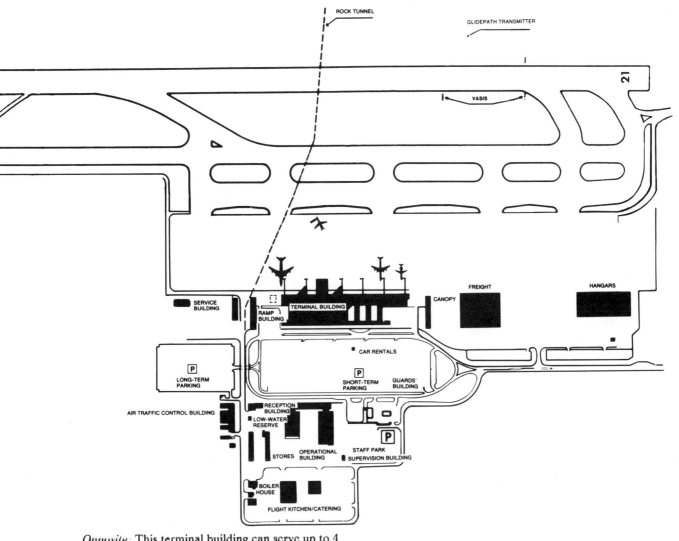

ROCK TUNNEL

GLIDEPATH TRANSMITTER

21

VASIS

SERVICE BUILDING

RAMP BUILDING

TERMINAL BUILDING

CANOPY

FREIGHT

HANGARS

CAR RENTALS

LONG-TERM PARKING

SHORT-TERM PARKING

GUARDS' BUILDING

AIR TRAFFIC CONTROL BUILDING

RECEPTION BUILDING

LOW-WATER RESERVE

STORES

OPERATIONAL BUILDING

STAFF PARK

SUPERVISION BUILDING

BOILER HOUSE

FLIGHT KITCHEN/CATERING

Opposite: This terminal building can serve up to 4 million passengers per year. Although the terminal is close to 1000 feet long by 300 feet wide, passengers need not walk more than 175 feet between the street and their planes. Passengers check in on street level, reach departure lounges by elevator or escalator, and board their flights via "nose bridges." The terminal houses a large number of facilities from shops, banks, post offices, cafeterias and restaurants to offices for airline companies and aviation administrators. *Above:* The backbone of a modern airport consists of its runway system, the site studied and evaluated to minimize noise. The prevailing wind conditions can be estimated to give a flight regularity of 99.5 percent. A runway 2 miles long will accommodate today's DC-10 and B-747 jets.

Airports in the decade following the war fought a losing
battle between updating terminals that were already
outmoded in the '30s and keeping up with the demands of
increasing numbers of passengers. By the early '50s, it
was clear that terminals for the forthcoming jet age
would require either a complete overhaul of existing
facilities or new sites entirely. *Above:* Stockholm's
Bromma Airport in 1953. *Opposite, top:* Los Angeles
Airport in 1947. *Opposite:* Elmo Bruner's Pueblo Revival
design for McCarren Field, Las Vegas, Nevada, 1948.

John F. Kennedy International Airport, New York.

International Arrivals Building at JFK.

British Airways Terminal at JFK.

American Airlines Terminal at JFK.

Eero Saarinen's Trans World Flight Center (TWA Terminal), John F. Kennedy International Airport, New York City, completed 1961. The terminal's soaring central structure suggests the flight of a great bird. The concrete shell, with its four interacting vaults, forms a huge protective umbrella over the passenger area. The two lateral vaults arch up into daring cantilevers. All the grace and beauty of flight are captured in the architect's sweeping design, a design calculated to stir in people the excitement and drama of air travel. As Aline B. Saarinen, the architect's widow, wrote in 1961: "Eero had a strong conviction that a building should be, as he put it, 'all one thing . . . that inside and outside should sing with the same message.' All the parts of the building—from stair-railings to the shape of signs—were studied like parts of a giant, unified piece of sculpture and were designed . . . with the hope that every part of the building would belong to 'one family of forms.'" Saarinen's "hope" was fully realized.

Kansas City International Airport, completed in 1972 and
designed by architects Kivett and Myers in association
with Burns & McDonnell Engineering Company, remains
the world's most imitated airport. Its "drive to your gate"
system involves much more than its aim alone: a walk of
no more than 75 feet from highway curb to boarding
gate. It is a completely integrated system that makes
possible decentralized passenger processing, baggage
handling, and automobile parking on an individual gate
position basis.

Newark International Airport's new terminals (1973).
Within a 425-acre oval arrangement are Terminals A and
B, each 800 by 165 feet and branching out to the three
satellite aircraft gate buildings. Each terminal has an
upper departure level with facilities for airline ticketing,
a lower arrival level for baggage claim and ground
transportation, and a ground parking level. A concourse,
halfway between upper and lower levels, has shops and
restaurants. *Left:* Newark's control tower.

Chicago-O'Hare International Airport, frequently called
the world's busiest, handles close to 50 million passengers
a year and just as many visitors. A total of 26 major
carriers, 7 commuter airlines, 4 supplemental carriers,
and 3 cargo carriers operate out of O'Hare on a regular
basis.

These views of Houston Intercontinental Airport should
be seen in conjunction with the photograph on p. 140.
The escalators from the concourse lead to the ample
parking lots around which the terminal is built.

Two roads, one above the other, separate automobile traffic from the arrival and departure floors of La Guardia Airport's curved terminal building, enclosed in glass and aluminum curtain walls. Completed in 1964, the improved La Guardia was designed by Harrison & Abramovitz.

A model of the new Baltimore Washington International Airport, built completely around a 30-year-old functioning terminal in order to serve a traveling public that has increased 400 percent since the 1950s.

Overleaf: Dulles International Airport, Chantilly, Virginia (1962). Eero Saarinen's greatest building consists of two rows of sixteen outward-sloping pillars supporting an enormous roof. Although the form of the building is based on the dynamics and tension of "take-off," the terminal is noted for the functional way it deals with the needs of airline traffic.

Three terminals in moderate-size American cities.
Above: The basic concept of the Jacksonville (Florida)
International Airport (1968) is unique in that enplaning
and deplaning passengers use opposite sides of the
terminal, a system that eliminates the passenger
congestion at most airports. *Opposite, top:* Memphis
(Tennessee) International Airport. *Opposite:* Norfolk
(Virginia) International Airport is, astonishingly, located
in the famous Norfolk Botanical Gardens and has been
nationally recognized for expanding its facilities without
disturbing the delicate ecological balance in the natural
woodland area.

Two of America's oldest and busiest jet-age
transportation complexes: Greater Pittsburgh
International Airport (*top*) and Los Angeles International
Airport. Los Angeles alone anticipates 40 million
passengers yearly by 1984.

San Jose (California) Municipal Airport.

Travelers visiting Dallas-Fort Worth International Airport agree that the terminal is more exciting an experience than their flights. The stark Buck Rogers quality of riding the automated trains between terminal buildings approximates the thrills that characterized aviation in its earliest days.

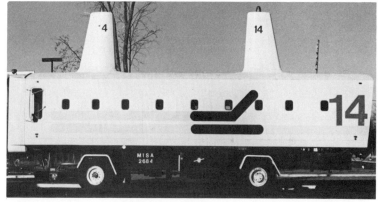

Mirabel, Montreal's international airport, is designed to be highly functional. One of its key services is the passenger transfer vehicle (PTV) which carries passengers between the terminal and the aircraft, saving long walks and providing operational advantages as well. PTVs make it unnecessary for aircraft to cluster around the terminal, thus preventing congestion and providing smoother service. PTVs carry 150 passengers and act as moving satellites of the aircraft.

Counterclockwise from opposite, top: Entry to Christchurch (New Zealand) Airport; Dunedin (New Zealand) Airport; Auckland (New Zealand) International Airport; a Quantas Boeing 747-B at Melbourne Airport, Tullamarine, Australia.

Top: Mexico City Airport. Older terminals can accommodate small jets if runways are sufficiently long. *Above:* Rendering of the Hellenic Aerospace Industry aircraft maintenance and manufacturing complex, Tanagra, Greece. Designed and constructed by The Austin Company for the Greek government, the complex is one of the major aviation-support facilities in the Mediterranean and includes hangars, shops, office buildings, concrete ramps, taxiways, roadways, and rail lines. The enormous complex will enable Greece to be independent in world aviation.

Rio de Janeiro's new International Airport (1977) follows the same concept of bringing the passenger directly to the airport used at Kansas City and at Dallas-Fort Worth. The terminals are aligned along an axis road; and, around a half-moon, the aircraft are handled in an efficient manner, minimizing passenger walking distance.

Overleaf: Against a backdrop of Tokyo International Airport at Haneda are seen Nagasaki Airport (*left*) and flight satellites at Tokyo's new Narita Airport.

A 1967 view of the organized chaos that is one of the world's busiest airports, London's Heathrow, now directly connected with the city by Underground. Loved by most tourists, it has been likened to Topsy, who just "growed."

Helsinki-Vantaa Airport is the center of Finnish air traffic. As the national airport, it handles the greatest part of international traffic to and from Finland. As a local airport, it serves the capital's 1.5 million residents.

Brussels International Airport, like JFK's International
Arrivals Building (p. 148), is unique in its height. See pp.
63-65 for nostalgic views.

A portion of the duty-free shop at Copenhagen Airport.
Tourists at such shops worldwide spend their last minutes
in a foreign country finding ways to spend the "strange"
currency still in their pockets.

Above: The Göteborg-Landvetter Airport (1977) is designed to handle 4 million travelers and 110,000 tons of freight a year. It should be compared with its predecessors of 1923 and 1940 on pp. 66-67.

Top: Stockholm's Arlanda International Airport (1976) was built to serve the 14 million passengers that are forecasted for the year 1990. As at many other terminals, passengers enter the departure hall on the upper level, and incoming passengers use the lower level.

Top: Ostend Airport, Middelkerke, Belgium, one of
hundreds of small municipal terminals serving European
cities.

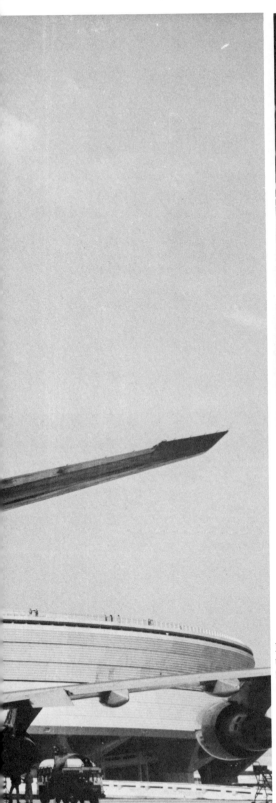

Paris's ultramodern Charles de Gaulle Airport was designed to be both functional and theatrical. Passengers are whisked through glass tubes (*above*) to "satellite stations" for boarding. The complex is so intriguing that delays here seem "briefer" than at any other airport. The terminal roof (*left*) is the biggest parking lot in Paris.

Top: Kloten Airport, Zurich, Switzerland.

Above: Architect's model, Cointrin Airport, Geneva, Switzerland.

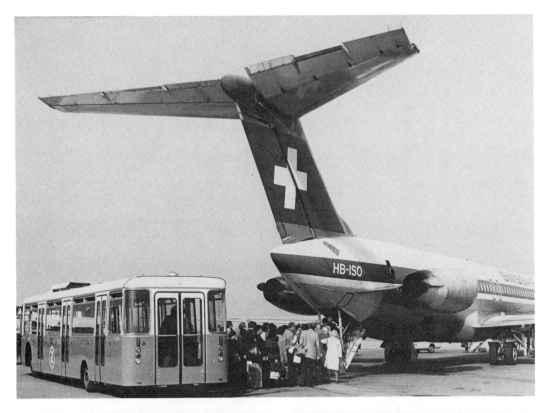

Top: Bus delivering passengers to aircraft from terminal at Cointrin.

Control tower, Cointrin Airport, Geneva.

The Rhine-Main Airport at Frankfurt, West Germany,
only eleven minutes from town by train.

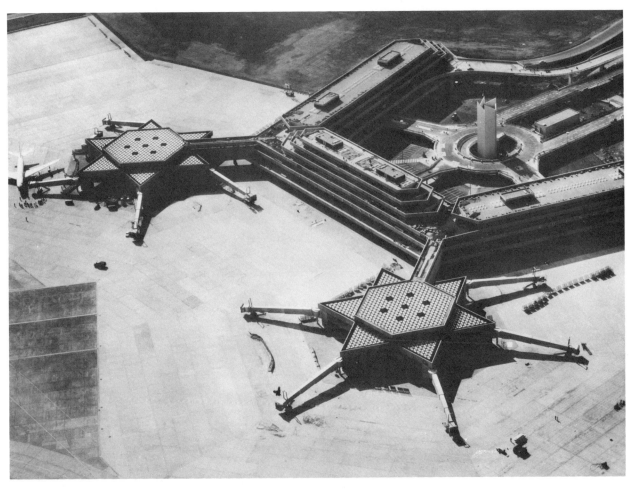

Star-shaped terminal satellites at the Cologne-Bonn
Airport, West Germany.

Above: A view of the eastern wing of Berlin's Tegel Airport and its free-standing control tower. Tegel, like every modern airport, is planned for heavy automobile traffic and incorporates ramps and roads connected to a maze of highway interchanges. *Opposite:* Tegel's passenger hall on opening day, 1974.

The airport:
Getting there is half the fun.

Credits

In this list of photographic credits, the following abbreviations are used: a (above), b (below), c (center), l (left), and r (right).

Jacket: American Airlines. *Frontispiece:* Trans World Airlines, an Ezra Stoller Associates photograph. *Contents page:* Ford Motor Company.

Preface: p. 6, author's collection.

Introduction: p. 10, Delta Air Lines; pp. 12-17, Atlanta Historical Society; p. 18, William B. Hartsfield-Atlanta International Airport.

Chapter 1: p. 24, The State Historical Society of North Dakota; p. 28, Ibid.; p. 29, Bishop Museum; pp. 30-31, Arizona Historical Society; p. 32, State Historical Society of North Dakota; p. 33 (a), Tourist and Convention Bureau, Pensacola, Florida; p. 33 (b), Aviation Department, Metropolitan Dade County, Florida; p. 34, Emory Tobin Collection in the Archives, University of Alaska, Fairbanks; p. 35, State Historical

Society of North Dakota; p. 36 (a), Kentucky Historical Society; p. 36 (b), Orange County Historical Museum; p. 37, Aviation Department, Metropolitan Dade County, Florida; pp. 38-39, Orange County Historical Museum; p. 39 (a, l), Kentucky Historical Society; p. 39 (a, r), The Annals of Iowa.

Chapter 2: p. 40, Bishop Museum; p. 43, author's collection; p. 44 (a), State Historical Society of Wisconsin; p. 44 (b), U.S. Air Force; p. 45, Nevada Historical Society; p. 46 (a), Naval Aviation Museum; p. 46 (b), U.S. Navy; p. 47, Naval Aviation Museum; pp. 48-49, Missouri Historical Society; p. 49 (a), Charles Bunnel Collection in the Archives, University of Alaska, Fairbanks; 49 (b), Glenbow-Alberta Institute; pp. 50-51 (map), author's collection; p. 50 (a), State Historical Society of North Dakota; p. 50 (b), Lulu Fairbanks

Collection in the Archives, University of Alaska, Fairbanks; p. 51 (c), Nevada Historical Society; p. 52, Pictorial Materials Collection, Grand Rapids Public Museum; p. 53 (a), Arizona Historical Society; 53 (b), Trans World Airlines; p. 54, Noel Wien Collection in the Archives, University of Alaska, Fairbanks; p. 55 (a), American Airlines; p. 55 (b), Dearborn Historical Museum.

Chapter 3: p. 56, author's collection; p. 60, French Embassy Press and Information Division; pp. 61-62, author's collection; p. 63, German Information Center; pp. 64-65, Sabena Belgian World airlines; p. 65 (a), Scandinavian Airlines System; p. 65 (b), Sabena Belgian World Airlines; pp. 66-67, Scandinavian Airlines System; pp. 68-69, Aviation Department, Metropolitan Dade County, Florida; p. 70-71, author's collection.

Chapter 4: pp. 72-81, Lehigh Portland Cement Company

Chapter 5: p. 82, The Austin Company; pp. 86-87, Missouri Historical Society; p. 88 (a), author's collection; pp. 88-89, The Austin Company; p. 89 (a), Ibid.; pp. 90-91, Trans World Airlines; p. 92, author's collection; p. 93 (a), Pictorial Materials Collection, Grand Rapids Public Museum; p. 93 (c), Eastern Washington State Historical Society; p. 93 (b), Aviation Department, Metropolitan Dade County, Florida; p. 94, R. S. Knowlson, Lou Holland Collection, Kansas City Museum; p. 95, Los Angeles Department of Airports; p. 96, The Wyoming State Archives and Historical Department; p. 97 (a), Washington State Historical Society; p. 97 (b), Kentucky Historical Society; pp. 98-99, The Port Authority of New York and New Jersey; p. 99 (a), Aviation Department, Metropolitan Dade County, Florida; pp. 100-101, The Austin Company; p. 100 (c), Hollywood-Burbank Airport; p. 101 (c), The Austin Company; pp. 102-103, author's collection; p. 104 (a), Michigan State Archives; p. 104 (b), author's collection; p. 105, Oregon Historical Society; pp. 106-107, Wichita Historical Museum Association; p. 108, American Airlines; p. 109 (l), The State Historical Society of Iowa; p. 109 (r), Michigan State Archives; pp. 110-11, The Austin Company; pp. 112-13, Aviation Department, Metropolitan Dade County, Florida; p. 112 (a, l), author's collection; p. 112 (a, r), Aviation Department, Metropolitan Dade County, Florida; p. 114 (a), author's collection; p. 114 (b), The Annals of Iowa; p. 115 (a), State Historical Society of North Dakota; p. 115 (b), New Mexico State Records Center and Archives; pp. 116-17, Trans World Airlines; pp. 118-19, Ibid.; p. 120 (a), State Historical Society of Missouri; p. 120 (b), Houston Metropolitan Research Center; pp. 120-21, Buffalo and Erie County Historical Society.

Chapter 6: p. 122, The Austin Company; p. 124 (a, l and r), Goodyear Tire and Rubber Co.,; p. 124 (b), The Austin Company; p. 125, author's collection; p. 126 (l), Ibid.; p. 126 (r, a and b), Goodyear Tire and Rubber Co.; pp. 127-31, author's collection.

Chapter 7: p. 132, U.S. Air Force; p. 134 (a), Ibid.; p. 134 (b), Glenbow-Alberta Institute; p. 135, Aviation Department, Metropolitan Dade County, Florida; pp. 136-37, Hollywood-Burbank Airport; p. 138, British Airways; p. 139, German Information Center.

Chapter 8: p. 140, Department of Aviation, City of Houston; pp. 144-45, Swedish Information Service; pp. 146-47, Board of Civil Aviation, Sweden; p. 147 (a), Los Angeles Department of Airports; p. 147 (b), Courtesy, Family of Elmo Bruner; p. 148 (a), The Port Authority of New York and New Jersey; p. 148 (b), Skidmore, Owings & Merrill Architects, an Ezra Stoller Associates photograph; p. 149 (a), British Airways; p. 149 (b), The Port Authority of New York and New Jersey; pp. 150-51, Trans World Airlines, Ezra Stoller Associates photographs; p. 152, Air Commerce Division, Aviation Department, Kansas City International Airport; p. 153, The Port Authority of New York and New Jersey; p. 154, City of Chicago Department of Aviation; p. 155, Houston Metropolitan Research Center; p. 156, Harrison & Abramovitz Architects, A Maris (ESTO) photograph; p. 157, State Aviation Administration, Maryland Department of Transportation; pp. 158-59, U.S. Department of Transportation; p. 160, Jacksonville Port Authority; p. 161 (a), Memphis-Shelby County Airport Authority, a Jim Hilliard photograph; p. 161 (b), Norfolk Port and Industrial Authority, a Lawrence S. Williams photograph; p. 162 (a), County of Allegheny Department of Aviation; 162 (b), Los Angeles Department of Airports; p. 163, Airport Department, City of San Jose, California; pp. 164-65, American Airlines; p. 165, Dallas-Fort Worth Airport; pp. 166-67, Transports Canada; p. 168, New Zealand Consulate General, New York; p. 169 (a), Quantas Airways; p. 169 (b), New Zealand Consulate General, New York; p. 170 (a), Mexican National Tourist Council; p. 170 (b), The Austin Company; p. 171, Varig Brazilian Airlines; pp. 172-73, Japan National Tourist Organization; p. 174 (a), British Airways; p. 174 (b), Finnair; p. 175 (a), Sabena Belgian World Airlines; p. 175 (b), Danish Tourist Board; pp. 176-77, Board of Civil Aviation, Sweden; p. 176 (a), Ibid.; p. 177 (a), Sabena Belgian Airlines; pp. 178-79, French Embassy Press and Information Division; p. 180 (a), Swiss National Tourist Office; pp. 180-81, Swissair; p. 181 (a), Ibid.; p. 181 (b), Swiss National Tourist Office; pp. 182-87, German Information Center.

Index